FORBIDDEN FAIRWAYS

AFRICAN AMERICANS AND THE GAME OF GOLF

Calvin H. Sinnette

Library of Congress Cataloging-in-Publication Data

Sinnette, Calvin H.
    Forbidden fairways : a history of African Americans and the game
of golf / by Calvin H. Sinnette.
        p.   cm.
    Includes bibliographical references and index.
    ISBN 1-886947-42-2
    1. Afro-American golfers—History. 2. Golf—United States—
History.   3. Discrimination in sports—United States—History.
I. Title.
    GV981.S55   1998
    796.352′089′96073—DC21   97-43791
                                                                    CIP

Sleeping Bear Press
121 South Main
P.O. Box 20
Chelsea, MI 48118
www.sleepingbearpress.com

Printed and bound in the United States

10 9 8 7 6 5 4 3 2 1

Golfers depicted in the title page sketch are (from left to right): Ted
Rhodes, John Shippen, Renee Powell, Charlie Sifford (standing), Bill
Spiller (seated), Lee Elder, and Tiger Woods. The child holding the
club's name is not known.

For my beloved wife, Elinor.

To the memory of Robert "Bob" King, who was convinced
that the story had to be told, and to the memories of
John Fenwick, Dr. Thomas Jones, and Orval White,
dear friends, golfing partners, and passionate devotees of the game.

Contents

Foreword

To those who play golf, it is a game of many possibilities. There is always the possibility that a bad shot will be followed by a good one, that a poorly played hole will be followed by a birdie. With those possibilities comes the hope that the worst round ever played can be followed by your best and, always, that a discouraging season will be followed by one that leads you to believe—if only briefly—that the mysteries of the game have been revealed. There are few golfers who have the skills of the expert, but all are filled with hope, and harbor the belief that their best game is always their next.

From the time golf first appeared on these shores sometime in the late 1700s, African Americans have had little chance or hope of being a real part of the game. Despite the inalienable rights of all men that are enshrined in the nation's founding documents, opportunities for African Americans to become involved in golf—except at the most menial level—were denied, obstructed, or curtailed. While it is shameful that it happened, it is not very surprising.

Also not very surprising is the indomitable will of those who chose to play in spite of the overwhelming odds against them. Little is known about the existence of African American men and women who, in spite of the indignities suffered, waged a ceaseless battle to make golf a part of their lives. Black history is filled with courageous people who stood firm in the face of injustice—and claimed their right—and so is *Forbidden Fairways*.

Being a golfer, a sports fan, and a proud African American, I had already learned about the perseverance of Charlie Sifford and Althea Gibson. Thanks to Calvin Sinnette's enlightening book—truly a pioneering effort—I am now acquainted with such unsung heroes as Joe Bartholomew, Ann Gregory, Ted Rhodes, Paris Brown, Bill Spiller, and John Shippen. Their experiences and achievements against the odds increase the sense of pride I have in the strength and determination of my African American heritage.

If you love golf, that romance will not diminish after reading this book. However, you will come to love the game in a different way and with a deeper understanding that we, too, have a rich heritage on the golf links.

I know I do.

Stedman Graham
May 1998

Preface

In August of 1993, two dear friends, Ina and Robert King, invited my wife and me to spend some time with them at their summer home in East Hampton on the eastern end of Long Island. Other than seeing each other at sporadic social events, it had been many years since we had been in each other's company for any significant length of time. We welcomed the opportunity to share their hospitality and catch up on each other's activities.

Since I had been Bob's classmate in college, I knew that he was a dyed-in-the-wool tennis buff. Shortly after arriving at their home, however, we were surprised to learn that he had been collecting historical material on African American tennis players for a number of years. In fact, he was ready to put his thoughts on the subject in writing. Knowing that I had been playing golf for many years, Bob suggested that I give consideration to doing something similar regarding the history of African American golfers. My response to the idea was not positive. I had just finished an unsuccessful manuscript and was most unwilling at the time to embark on a new writing venture.

Despite my reluctance, though, the subject never left my subconscious and from time to time I would scribble a few ideas. The following summer, we were once again houseguests of Ina and Bob. By that time I was more receptive to Bob's persuasions and I began to warm to the notion of taking a stab at the project. After another delightful stay on Long Island, I returned home eager to start a line of historical research vastly different to any of my previous efforts. Of course, the subject dealt with a sport I truly loved and I was rather excited to see what might be uncovered.

Within days of my initial information-gathering efforts it became clear that a serious study of black golf history had never been written. To my surprise, I learned this after visiting the Library of Congress (LC). Justifiably proud of being the largest library in the world, the LC has more than nineteen million books in its collection. About

1,900 are golf-related. Though many contain short references to African American participation, only two were identified that examine the subject in any detail. In 1988, the late tennis champion, Arthur Ashe, succeeded in publishing *A Hard Road to Glory*. An ambitious undertaking, Ashe's three-volume work covers the participation of black athletes in a wide range of sports. However, only five pages in the first volume and eleven pages in the third are dedicated to golf. The other book, published in 1993, was *Just Let Me Play*, an autobiographical treatment of the career of golfer Charlie Sifford. Valuable as both books are, neither was intended to provide a detailed examination of African American golf history. This meant that I had to look for a source of information other than books. Fortunately, I found one.

Until recently, mainstream white newspapers seldom published substantive reports about developments in the African American community. This certainly happened in relation to golf. Were it not for the existence of the black press, it would have been extremely difficult, if not impossible, to trace the history of black golf. Not only did those accounts in the black newspapers provide information about what took place, but they also defined the social and cultural contours of the events. The black press became my guide and opened the broad vistas of black golf history to my vision.

As many of us know, the painful ironies of life are always lying in wait beyond the horizon. Two days before the contract for this book was completed, my dear friend Bob King passed away after a long, majestic struggle.

I hope that I have done justice to his strong belief that this story was worth telling.

Calvin Sinnette

Introduction: Unrequited Love

In the April 15, 1984 issue of *The New York Times*, a freelance writer named Michael Dixon wrote an account of a painful experience he had experienced as an African American playing the game of golf. Plaintively entitled "On Being Black and Loving Golf," the article describes a 1979 incident at Winged Foot Country Club in Mamaroneck, New York, that introduced Dixon to golfdom's racial animus. A few months prior to the incident, Dixon had played the course during the United States Golf Association's Media Day for the 1980 U. S. Senior Open and he'd had an enjoyable time. Much to his surprise, though, when he attempted to play in a *Golf* magazine outing at Winged Foot later in the year, he was told by one of the magazine's senior editors that "someone had a problem" with his previous presence on the course. The editor never mentioned who had the "problem" or what the nature of the "problem" was, but the message was clear: the editor wanted him to reconsider his intention of participating in the event. Realizing that he was not welcome, Dixon withdrew.

Four years later, a former colleague of Dixon's who was a new member at the prestigious Merion Golf Club in Philadelphia was told to "Forget it" when he mentioned that he wanted to invite a black friend to play the course. Of this latest incident Dixon wrote, "I wasn't going down to Merion to stage a demonstration, challenge their membership rules, or marry the club president's daughter. I just wanted to play a golf course I'd heard and read and dreamed about. And I couldn't. Because I'm black." Expressing his contempt for those who prevented him from enjoying a round of golf he felt he would long remember, Dixon continued, "Broken down to its most basic element, golf is just a person, a club, a ball, and a shot to be played. None of that has anything to do with the color of anyone's skin. And yet in the real world of golf, it seems often to have everything to do with it." The journalist had mixed feelings about the future, and concluded by stating, "In a way, I'd like to say 'forget it,' and never play again. That isn't likely because [I'd miss] the game terribly. But if I did, golf would lose one of its best friends it never knew it had."

Every time I read "On Being Black and Loving Golf," Dixon's words resonate within my being. They bring back a hurtful golf-related incident that happened to me a number of years ago.

One spring in the late 1950s, I went with a group of friends to Grossinger's Hotel in the Catskill Mountains north of New York City for a weekend of golf. We had planned the event since early winter and, as the date approached, we looked forward with eagerness to our first outing of the year. In the group was an assortment of lawyers, dentists, businessmen, and physicians, all of whom shared a passion for golf and the camaraderie associated with the game. We had no illusions about breaking par but we clung to the dream that our sojourn would usher in a new season of pleasurable golf in an idyllic setting.

Because of unexpected delays, we did not arrive at the resort until late Friday afternoon. We had hoped to play at least nine holes before nightfall, but our late arrival prevented us from playing that afternoon. By the time we checked into our rooms on the hotel's top floor and got settled, it was time to get ready for dinner. After shaving, showering, and changing into suitable dinner attire, we met as a group at the bank of elevators on our floor. Four of us entered the car that was heading down to the dining room. Two floors down, the elevator stopped to admit additional passengers.

When the doors opened, two elderly white women stepped in. Visibly taken aback to find themselves in close quarters with a group of black men (those were the days when we referred to ourselves as Negroes), each of the women gave a short, soft, but distinctly audible gasp. Their eyes darted about and their lips quivered as they tried to maintain their composure. The elevator doors closed and the car renewed its descent. At this point, the more intrepid of the two women looked at us with a tentative smile and asked, "Do you boys play in the band?" The looks on our faces betrayed a mixture of perplexity, anger, disgust, and resignation.

Even though we were well-groomed, well-behaved, and fairly prosperous-looking, it was all lost on the two women. They had defined, classified, and assigned us our roles with astonishing ease, speed, and self-confidence. Skin color was the sole criterion they used to infer that we were the house musicians. That we might take umbrage at being referred to as "boys" never crossed their minds. Once again blind, irrational racial stereotyping was the order of the day. It was one helluva way to start a weekend of golf.

Yet, my unforgettable experience at Grossinger's pales in comparison to the abasement and crude indignities suffered on golf courses over the years by the Charlie Siffords, Ann Gregorys, Bill Spillers, Renee Powells, and countless other African Americans. Nevertheless, despite the grudging and agonizingly slow pace of improvement in the attitude and behavior of the dominant culture, one cannot deny that favorable changes have taken place. With each passing year, the situation for African American golfers has become more hopeful. Another important milestone was reached in the waning days of the 1996 summer season with the spectacular arrival of Eldrick "Tiger" Woods on the world's golf scene. His presence has the potential to drive another mighty nail into the moldering coffin of racial prejudice. Its burial is long overdue.

1 | When the Word Was Given

It is most unlikely that we shall ever discover the identity of the first African American to swing a golf club on the North American mainland. Regarded by the ruling society as marginal at best, the first blacks to strike a golf ball mattered little to those who introduced the game on the shores of colonial America. They saw no reason to document who those black people were. Nevertheless, there is evidence to suggest that the event probably occurred in the latter half of the eighteenth century on the South Carolina coast. By that time, the city of Charleston was a thriving commercial center with an unusual abundance of social and cultural activities. A large number of the merchant class were transplanted Scotsmen and Englishmen who brought their passion for golf with them when they crossed the Atlantic. By 1786, they were instrumental in establishing the South Carolina Golf Club in Charleston, acknowledged today by many authorities to be the first golf club in the United States.

Hunting was a popular pastime among slave owners during the colonial era and they frequently took their bonded servants with them on hunting trips. The slaves were given the laborious (and sometimes dangerous) task of flushing animals into the open, retrieving downed fowls, and skinning the game that had been killed.(1) In *The Carolina Lowcountry Birthplace of American Golf*, authors Charles Price and George C. Rogers, Jr. surmise that the slaves were similarly assigned the onerous duties associated with the game of golf. They speculate that slaves were used as caddies by members of the South Carolina Golf Club. Although there are no records to substantiate the authors' conjecture, from what is known of slave life, there is ample reason to support their assumption that African Americans were involved with the game of golf from its earliest beginnings on these shores.

Over the next few decades, golf enjoyed a fair degree of popularity in both South Carolina and Georgia. At Savannah Golf Club, founded in 1796, as well as at South Carolina GC, slaves probably were used for two main purposes. Since there were no greens as we know of them today, the slaves were used as "finders." In this role they were required to determine the position of the hole and mark it with a suitable object so that an upcoming player would know its location. The South Carolina Golf Club played the game on Harleston Green, a public park in the center of Charleston that was also used by other city inhabitants for horse races, cricket matches, picnicking, and strolling. The second important responsibility entrusted to the slaves was to yell "Fore" to alert other park users of an approaching shot. At the end of the game, these fore caddie/slaves undoubtedly were given the golf clubs to clean, polish, and store while the slave owner rested and enjoyed refreshments. It was an ideal, but probably perilous, opportunity for a slave to secretly test his master's golf equipment. Considering human nature, it would be naive to think otherwise.

For reasons not thoroughly understood, golf's popularity with the South Carolinians and Georgians began to wane by the end of the second decade of the nineteenth century. Some believe it was due to the War of 1812 and the resulting decline in shipping, both of which led many of the Scotsmen and Englishmen to return home. Others attribute the decrease in popularity around Charleston to an encroachment of new buildings into Harleston Green, thereby depriving the golfers of the space they needed to play. Whatever the reasons, golf virtually disappeared from the American sporting scene. It led one golf historian to observe, "From 1811 till a much disputed date in the middle eighties, America had practically no golf at all, at least there is no trace of any having been played, and these seventy-five years can truthfully be said to be the dark ages of the Scottish game in this country. What seed was planted in the eighteenth century never took deep root." (2)

Those 75 years may have been the "dark ages" of golf in the

United States, but it was also the period during which African Americans were unshackled from bondage. From the slave's vantage point, even one who might have learned to enjoy the game, there was no question that the freedom ushered in by the Emancipation Proclamation of 1863 was a far more cherished commodity than playing golf.

While player participation in the United States was in a period of decline, other developments were taking place in the sport that would later have a significant impact on its popularity. The first of these events was the introduction in Scotland and England of the gutta-percha ball in 1848. Until then, golf balls were made of stitched leather that was stuffed with feathers. Referred to as "featheries," they tended to soften and/or unravel easily and often had to be replaced during the course of play. On the other hand, gutta-percha, the latex sap of the Malaysian sapodilla tree, could be molded into a hard sphere that retained its shape much longer than its predecessor. Moreover, the "guttie" could be manufactured cheaply, thereby permitting the game to become more accessible to the working class population.

In the 1890s, other events occurred which rekindled American interest in golf. By 1896, Albert G. Spalding had begun large-scale manufacturing and selling of golf clubs. About the same time, George Wright, an importer of golf equipment from England, started to promote the sport by petitioning the Boston Parks Commissioner for a permit giving him " . . . the privilege to play in Franklin Park the game of golf."(3) A year earlier, Van Cortlandt Park Golf Course, the nation's first public golf facility, opened in the Riverdale section of New York City's borough of The Bronx. Thomas Bendelow, the Scottish-born architect who designed the course, was a former employee of the Spalding Company. In the fourth year after the course opened, 1,892 permits were issued for golfers to line up on the first tee.(4) It was evident that golf was regaining its appeal and was now coming into its own as a popular American sport —one that African Americans would also begin to play in gradually increasing numbers.

2 | Five Trailblazers of the Nineteenth and Twentieth Centuries

George Grant

While there are no known records to verify the identities of any black golfers during *colonial* times, there is considerable evidence that George Franklin Grant was one of the earliest African American golfers in the post-Civil War era.

Over 150 years have passed since two proud African American parents gazed upon their newborn son. They had recently escaped from Southern bondage and were looking forward with great anticipation to raising their family away from the slave master's whiplash. The name they gave to the baby was George. He was born on September 15, 1846 in the small town of Oswego, New York, and he was one of seven children born to Phillis Pitt and Tudor Elandor Grant. (1)

After completing elementary school, young George left home to make his way in the world. Quite by chance, the youngster began working for a hometown dentist; first as an errand boy and later, after showing his ability, as an assistant in his employer's dental laboratory. In 1867, with great enthusiasm but virtually no financial resources, he moved to Boston, Massachusetts. Once again he obtained employment as a dental laboratory assistant. The following year, demonstrating both technical skills and determination, the

1870 Dental school graduation photograph of
Dr. George Grant.
(Credit: Harvard Medical Library)

twenty-two-year-old managed to gain entrance to the newly established Harvard Dental School. Working part-time, George scraped
together enough money to complete the two-year dental course. In
1870, he graduated with honors as the second-ranking student in his
class. His was the second class to finish at the new institution, and he
was its second African American graduate.(2)

Within four years, Dr. George Grant was awarded a position on
the Harvard dental faculty, primarily because of his excellent work
with patients who were born with a defect in the roof of the mouth.
Referred to as having a congenital cleft palate, these patients invari-

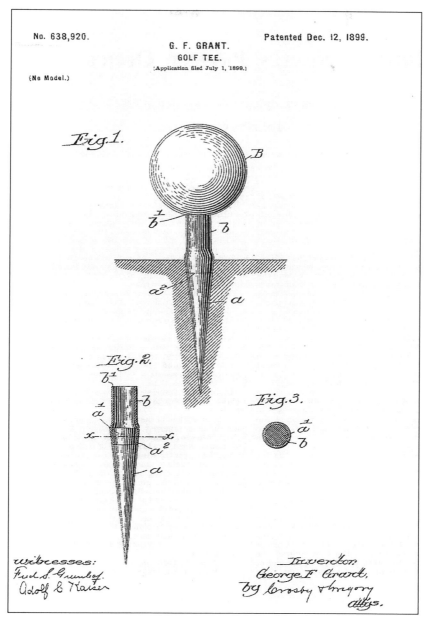

No. 638,920.

G. F. GRANT.
GOLF TEE.
(Application filed July 1, 1899.)

Patented Dec. 12, 1899.

(No Model.)

Fig.1.

Fig.2.

Fig.3.

Witnesses:
Fred S. Greenleaf.
Adolf E. Kaiser

Inventor:
George F. Grant,
by Crosby & Gregory
attys.

U.S. Patent Office sketch drawing of Grant's invention, the first tee.

ably have difficulty with eating and speaking. Using his considerable manual dexterity, Grant fashioned individually-fitted artificial palates for the patients to use. Within a short time, his professional stature had grown to the extent that he was recognized by colleagues in the United States and abroad. In addition to his work with cleft palate patients, Grant was a competent general dentist. Many of his patients were members of prominent Boston families, and he was consulted by individuals living as far away as Michigan and New Brunswick, Canada.

It is not known when this black Boston dentist began playing golf, but his daughter, Frances, recalled caddying for him in the mid-1880s. A nearby meadow served as the golf course. At that time, the Grant family was living in Arlington Heights, a Boston suburb. By 1890, after encountering racial discrimination in the housing market, Grant succeeded in buying a house at 108 Charles Street in Boston's Beacon Hill district.(3) The new residence was well suited for his large dental practice, but Grant continued to keep the Arlington Heights property. It was his outlet for golf and whenever his patient schedule and the weather permitted, he would head for Arlington Heights. There, on the adjacent meadowland "course," he would play with his three golfing companions: Archibald Grimke, the noted civil rights leader, lawyer, editor, and consular official; Butler Wilson, an 1884 Boston Law School graduate; and Howard Lee, a well-known Boston restaurateur. Frances Grant further recalled that "Golf courses were rather primitive in those days; just a big open meadow. All you had to do was worry about the cows . . . "(4)

During this era, primitive golf courses were commonplace. Observing the golfing conditions prevalent at the turn of the century, one writer noted, "The few courses established then were built by folks who could afford the sport—golf was strictly a rich man's game . . . Deprived of country club links, [the less wealthy] players resorted to empty meadows."(5) In some quarters it was referred to as "petty links" golf. If it was difficult for the average middle- or working-class white golfer to find a suitable course to play, it was immeasurably more difficult for the African American golfer, regardless of income, education, or class. Grant and his playing companions, therefore, could consider themselves fortunate to have access to the Arlington Heights meadowland.

Until George Franklin Grant decided to do something about it, golfers in the last decade of the nineteenth century teed up their balls on small mounds of damp sand which they had pinched into shape with their fingers. Annoyed with having to follow this procedure at every tee box (literally, a box full of sand next to the teeing area), Grant decided to fashion a wooden peg to support the ball. On December 12, 1899, the United States Patent Office issued patent number 638,920 to George F. Grant for the device he had invented. It was the first golf tee registered by the Patent Office. The official record states, "This invention has for its objectives the production of a simple, cheap and effective tee for use in the game of golf, obviating the use of conical mounds of sand or similar material, formed by the fingers of the player on which the ball is supported when teeing off." Recognizing that the device would assist the golfer to achieve a greater degree of consistency, the record states further that "By use of the tee . . . the player is sure that his ball is uniformly elevated from the ground and the uncertainty of the sand tee is overcome, as it is practically impossible to make them of uniform height each time."

The Patent Office's official description reads:

Claim 1. An article of manufacture, a golf-tee comprising a tapering portion to be driven into the ground point first, and a flexible tubular head, the lower end of which embraces the upper portion of the base. Claim 2. An article of manufacture, a golf-tee comprising a tapering base portion adapted to be inserted in the ground point first and having a shoulder near its upper end, a tubular head, the lower end of which embraces the tapering base portion above the shoulder.(6)

Grant had the tees manufactured by a small shop in Arlington Heights, and he kept bags of them in various places in both of his houses. His daughter recalled the clutter of golf tees and commented that she and her friends " . . . played with them as we might play with jacks." She also noted that Grant himself, "just kept the things around the house and handed them out to friends as he would a stick of candy." Busy as he was with his dental practice, his academic responsibilities at the dental school, and his civic duties on behalf of

Boston's African American community, Grant never marketed his wooden golf tee for commercial gain. He made a comfortable living for himself and his family from his profession, and he did not seek to profit from his invention. His daughter observed: "He loved challenges, but once he overcame them, he lost interest and moved on to something else."

Twenty-five years after Grant received his official patent office registration number, Dr. William Lowell, a white golfer from New Jersey who was also a dentist, obtained patent number 1,497,687 for a golf tee he had invented. In contrast to his black dental colleague in Boston, Lowell exploited the commercial potential of his invention. He paid $1,500 to U. S. Open champion Walter Hagen and trickshot artist Joe Kirkwood to promote his device. They helped to popularize the "new" golf tee and soon its use became widespread. For many years, not surprisingly, Lowell was considered to be the original inventor of the golf tee and Grant's contribution went unrecognized. Only through the persistence of Wornie L. Reed, an African American faculty member of the University of Massachusetts, did the United States Golf Association (USGA) acknowledge in 1991 that Grant was indeed the person who deserved recognition for receiving the first patent.(7)

George Grant died at his New Hampshire vacation home on August 21, 1910.

Walter Speedy

Although golf was penetrating rapidly into the sporting consciousness of white America, it was slow to catch on among the post-Civil War generation of African Americans (George Grant and his playing companions were exceptions). Before the turn of the century, golf was seldom, if ever, mentioned in the country's black newspapers. But as far back as 1880, news pertaining to tennis appeared in the black press. That year, an issue of *The New York Age* contained a short notice:

> The Yorkville Tennis Club will hold its first meeting of the season on Monday evening, May 21, at the residence of Paul G.

Barnwell, Jr., the president and manager, 219 East 88th Street.(8)

In the first volume of *A Hard Road to Glory*—a three-volume study of the African American athlete—Arthur Ashe observes that before 1900, boxing, track and field, horse racing, and cycling were the sports with the greatest following in the African American community. It comes as no surprise, then, that three decades would pass between the birth of George Grant and that of Walter Speedy, a little-known but important figure in the annals of African American golf.

Speedy was born in 1878 in Concordia Parish, Louisiana, some 65 miles east of the city of Alexandria.(9) Little is known about his early life, although it is suspected that he began playing golf (probably as a caddie) in the Bayou State before he migrated north. In 1909, nine years after he arrived in Chicago, he married Nettie George, a society reporter for the *Chicago Defender* newspaper. The couple had one known child, a daughter.

In 1910, when the city of Chicago held its public links golf tournament at Jackson Park Golf Course, Speedy and three other black players were barred from entry. Undaunted, the four men pooled their financial resources, engaged a lawyer and then sued park officials for not allowing them to play. The exact outcome of the litigation is unclear but it seems the court provided a measure of relief.

In 1915, Walter Speedy, Henry Johnson, Needham Wright, and Theodore Pankey were the nucleus of a group that formed the Alpha Golf Club. On October 7th of that year, the Alphas held the first African American golf tournament in Chicago history at Marquette Park Golf Course. One newspaper claimed that players from coast to coast took part in the one-day affair held on a blustery fall day that threatened snow. Speedy won the event and, together with three of the other top black finishers, was invited to play the best white player from Jackson Park.(10) Later events were to prove that the 1915 invitation was only a temporary goodwill gesture, and that it did not reflect a fundamental reversal of the policy of racial discrimination in place at the city's public golf courses.

In 1921, Walter Speedy found himself embroiled once again in a dispute with Chicago's Parks Department because of its unwilling-

ness to discontinue segregation. When the annual citywide tournament was announced the year before, Speedy and a group of other
black golfers registered for the event. When the men arrived at the
tournament (they were now organized as the Windy City Golf Association), they learned that their names had been erased from the registration book and had been replaced with the names of white
golfers. Although only Chicago residents were supposed to be eligible to play, Jackson Park GC (the tournament host) permitted two
white non-residents to enter while it excluded members of the
Windy City Golf Association. Speedy and his associates attempted to
obtain an injunction, but the presiding judge refused to grant the request on the grounds that not all of the Park Commissioners were
able to attend the hearing. The ruling was appealed in Circuit Court,
but the request for an injunction was again denied. The appellate
judge intimated that Windy City's grievances were justified but, because the petition had not been properly served, he could not rule in
its favor.(11) The unsavory incident prompted a *Chicago Defender*
sportswriter to comment, "Through one pretext or another our folks
have been barred from competition in tournament play in Jackson
Park. Primarily it is claimed [that] the Jackson Park Golf Club has
been responsible for this latest form of jim-crowism . . ." With
tongue in cheek, the writer concluded: ". . . it is barely possible if
they [the black golfers] were not quite so good this senseless opposition would be less pronounced."(12)

The following year, the *Chicago Defender* newspaper sponsored its
first and only golf tournament. Billed as a "national" golf event, it
was emphasized that all amateurs, regardless of race, creed, or color
were allowed to enter. The Windy City Golf Association directed the
tournament and Walter Speedy was listed among the participants.

In addition to maintaining an active social calendar, Walter and
Nettie Speedy were enthusiastic baseball fans. They maintained a box
behind home plate at the ball field of the American Giants, a local
African American baseball team. The Speedys regularly attended the
team's home games and frequently had out-of-town visitors as their
guests at the old 39th Street baseball diamond.

Always at the forefront of championing the cause of black golfers,
Speedy readily understood the value of a national organization that
would address the needs and concerns of the African American golf-

ing community. After meeting Robert Hawkins of Boston, it was only a matter of time before the two kindred spirits began to lay the groundwork for such an enterprise. Within a matter of months, the two men found others who shared their interest and vision. In late 1925, under the determined and energetic leadership of the two men, the United States Colored Golf Association came into existence. The following year it staged its first open golf tournament at the Mapledale Country Club in Stow, Massachusetts.(13) The event was such a resounding success that Speedy, gratified by the response of his fellow black golfers, felt confident that the new organization would usher in a new era for the black golfing public.

Speedy continued to remain active in matters regarding golf throughout the 1930s. He officiated at many of the national black golf tournaments and for years he was an active supporter of, and mentor to, the Chicago Women's Golf Club. In 1942, when George May permitted black golfers to participate in the Tam O' Shanter national tournaments that he sponsored, Walter Speedy was appointed to the committee to select the African American participants. Referred to by some as "the father of golf in Chicago," Speedy enjoyed the respect and admiration of African American golfers across the country.

On November 9, 1943, Speedy became ill with pneumonia. When his condition worsened over the next week, he was moved to Provident Hospital where he died on November 21st. Following a funeral service in Chicago, his body was taken to Springfield, Ohio, for interment. After his death, the Chicago Women's Golf Club renamed its annual event the Walter Speedy Memorial Tournament in honor of the man who was instrumental in bringing the organization into existence.

John Shippen

The year following Walter Speedy's birth, another golfer of African descent, the legendary John Matthew Shippen, Jr., was born in Washington, D. C. He was the first golf professional to be born in the United States, and to this date he has not been accorded his rightful place in the pantheon of America's golf heroes. When he died in 1968, Shippen had languished in virtual obscurity for more than 40 years.

One early substantive description of Shippen's life appeared in the March, 1957, issue of *Golfing* magazine. Written by Frank Strafaci, a well-known amateur golfer in the metropolitan New York City area, the article characterized Shippen as the "Forgotten Pioneer Professional." Strafaci had gone to great lengths to locate Shippen, and when he found him living at 204 Plainfield Avenue in Scotch Plains, New Jersey, he was struck by the seventy-eight-year-old's remarkable agility and rhythmic golf swing. At the time of the interview, Shippen observed tactfully, "There are many magnificent golfers today playing a different game than was played in the early days . . . But the golfers of yesterday and today you can compare. As great as today's players are, they're no better in skill, finesse, and competitive heart than such fellows as Alex Smith, Willie Anderson, Jerry Travers, and Walter Travis. I think it's reasonable to say that if they could have played under today's conditions, they'd beat today's stars."(14)

Twelve years passed before another fairly lengthy account of Shippen's life was published, this time by W. Leonard Evans, Jr., the African American president and editor of *Tuesday* publications. Evans saw to it that an extensive article on Shippen's exceptional career was published in his popular magazine supplement for the black press.(15) In the article, the author took great pains to correct some of the errors of fact about Shippen that had been written by others.

In 1973, four years after the article was first published, Evans, an ardent golfer and successful entrepreneur, hosted the *Tuesday* Pro Am Invitational Tournament at the Prince Georges Country Club in Landover, Maryland. For the event, Evans prepared a handsome souvenir program which contained a reprint of the 1969 article in its entirety. "As a pioneer," Evans wrote in the introductory statement, "in a sport where there have been fewer opportunities to develop the competitive edge necessary to excel, he [Shippen] can be a beacon of hope and inspiration for present and future golfers." Evans recognized Shippen's important contributions to golf, and he looked upon the tournament as a part of the Shippen legacy. Concluding, perhaps prophetically, Evans wrote, "We are certain that one day, in a future era, a John Shippen will emerge to not only take the lead in the U. S. Open but go on to become the U. S. Open Champion and thus fulfill the dream of this stalwart golf pioneer."

Unfortunately, in the attempt to provide an increased measure of recognition to John Shippen, a number of incorrect statements were written about him. For instance, even the otherwise accurate 1969 *Tuesday* article stated that Shippen was born in 1878. The census records of 1880, however, reveal that this isn't true. John Matthew Shippen, Jr. was born on December 5, 1879, the fourth of nine children in the family of John Matthew, Sr. and Eliza Spotswood Shippen.(16) At the time of the boy's birth, the Shippen family lived on Nichols Avenue in the Hillsdale section of Washington, D. C.'s Anacostia neighborhood.

Seven years previously, Shippen's father had received a "certificate of satisfactory study" from the Preparatory Department at Howard University which enabled him to become an elementary teacher in the Washington Public School System. He taught for a number of years but returned to Howard for religious training, and graduated with a diploma in theology in 1883. Needing greater financial remuneration than that provided in the public schools, the elder Shippen was ordained in the Presbyterian Church and left teaching to accept minor church positions in Fayetteville, Arkansas and Florence, Alabama.(17)

In 1888, Reverend John Shippen, Sr. was assigned to the Presbyterian mission on the Shinnecock Indian reservation in Southampton on New York's Long Island. He arrived at the local railroad station at the height of that year's famous blizzard. When he was installed as pastor in early 1889, he sent for his family. Then 10 years old, John, Jr. fitted readily into the routines of his Shinnecock playmates. He went to school, fished, swam, and rode horses with them. In the process he became a close friend of Oscar Bunn, a member of a well-known Shinnecock family.

Two years after the Shippens moved to the reservation, a group of wealthy Southampton summer residents bought 80 acres nearby on a narrow stretch of land between Peconic Bay on the north and the Atlantic Ocean on the south. The intent of the new owners was to build a golf course that would equal the best of the renowned British seaside links. To supervise the construction, the new club owners hired William Davis, a highly-regarded Scots golfer who had recently arrived in the United States. Davis tapped the adjoining reservation for labor and built the original 12-hole course. When Davis left a year later, in 1895, he was replaced by fellow-Scotsman Willie Dunn. After he turned the course into an 18-hole layout, Dunn began to teach some of the local youth to caddie. Among his more promising students were John Matthew Shippen, Jr. and Oscar Bunn.

Soon all thoughts of completing their education vanished as Shippen and Bunn became thoroughly captivated by the game. Shippen spent every waking moment on the golf course practicing under the watchful eye of Willie Dunn. He proved to be such a talented pupil that Dunn made him an assistant and permitted him to give lessons to some of the club members. Described as short and wiry, Shippen was known to have "a vicious swing." Charlie Thom, a Shinnecock club professional, observed, "I've never seen anything like it, yet he could control his club as if he had it on a string."(18)

In addition to instructing, Shippen served as a starter for tournaments, repaired clubs, and assisted the maintenance staff. Gradually it became evident that Shippen's skill as a golfer warranted an opportunity for the sixteen-year-old caddie to match his prowess with the top-ranked golfers of the day. That opportunity came in 1896 when Shinnecock Hills was selected by the United States Golf Association to be the site of the second U. S. Open Championship. Encouraged by club members who were convinced of his talents, Shippen decided to enter along with his friend Oscar Bunn. But before he could step onto the first tee, Shippen had to do battle with, and defeat, the plague of racism that has faced each generation of African American golfers.

The exact circumstances surrounding the racial incident remain somewhat vague, but certain facts have emerged that are beyond dispute. The day before the Open was to begin, a number of the entrants, mostly English and Scottish professionals, confronted Theodore F. Havemeyer, the tournament director and first USGA president, and threatened to withdraw if Shippen and Bunn were allowed to play. To his everlasting credit, Havemeyer informed the players that the tournament would be played as scheduled, even if it meant that Shippen and Bunn were the only contestants. According to other accounts of the incident, Havemeyer is alleged to have stated that Shippen was only "half black," implying that he would have prohibited the minister's son from playing if he were a full-blooded African American.(19) Regardless of what actually was said during the discussions, Havemeyer's uncompromising stand forced the protesters to abandon their walkout. The tournament began the following morning before an expectant gallery.

Playing with deliberate concentration, Shippen vindicated the claims of his supporters. He demonstrated for all to see that despite being the youngest of the players, he possessed the skills of a seasoned veteran. In the first round of the two-day event he shot a 78, which placed him in a tie for first place with four other players. His playing partner was Charles B. Macdonald, the designer of Chicago Golf Club and a highly regarded golfer who had won the first U. S. Amateur Championship at Newport Country Club in Rhode Island the year before. Thoroughly dissatisfied when he carded an 83 in the opening round, Macdonald withdrew in a fit of pique. Coincidentally, Shippen's first day's score was identical to that of his former mentor, Willie Dunn, who had left Shinnecock Hills earlier that year to become the club professional at the Ardsley Club in Westchester, New York.

The next day, Shippen played the first nine holes with steady precision. Midway through the incoming nine, though, disaster struck. On the 13th hole, his drive landed in a sandy waste on the right-hand side and he took a horrendous eleven strokes to recover. At the end of the tournament, Shippen was tied for fifth place with a combined score of 159—seven strokes behind James Foulis, the winner. For his efforts, John Shippen collected ten dollars and became the first African American to earn money as a contestant in a U. S. Open. His nightmarish performance on the 13th hole, however, haunted Shippen for the remainder of his life. The previously mentioned *Tuesday* magazine article quoted Shippen's recollection of the misfortune that befell him on that summer afternoon in 1896. "It was a little, easy par four. I'd played it many times and I knew I just had to stay on the right side of the fairway with my drive. Well, I played it too far to the right and the ball landed in a sand road. Bad trouble in those days before sand wedges. I kept hitting the ball along the road, unable to lift it out of the sand, and wound up with an unbelievable eleven for the hole. You know, I've wished a hundred times I could have played that little par four again. It sure would have been something to win that day."

Even though he failed in his quest to win the Open, Shippen's impressive performance caught the attention of many observers, including members of Maidstone Club, which was about to open in nearby East Hampton. An invitation was extended to America's first native-born golf professional to play an exhibition match of two 18-hole rounds against R. B. Wilson, the new golf professional at Shinnecock Hills. Before a large audience, Shippen defeated Wilson. The event was reported in a leading sports magazine of the day with an unusual degree of open-mindedness and candor:

A good match was played at Shinnecock Hills between the two professionals, Wilson and Shippen. The scores were:

Mr. Shippen
Out . . . 5 5 4 4 3 5 5 4 7   In . . . 5 4 4 6 5 5 4 4 4—83
Mr. Wilson
Out . . . 4 4 3 4 4 4 5 5 6   In . . . 6 4 3 4 5 6 4 5 5—81

Second Round

Mr. Shippen
Out . . . 5 4 4 4 4 4 5 3 6   In . . . 5 5 3 3 5 5 4 4 5—78
Mr. Wilson
Out . . . 4 5 4 3 4 5 7 6 6   In . . . 5 3 4 5 5 5 4 4 5—84

Shippen won this very close and remarkably well-played match by 2 up and 1 to play. Shippen's second round is the best 18 holes yet played in this country by an American born. He was a caddie at Shinnecock Hills, but now ranks as one of the best professionals in the country. It is hoped that Shippen will be enabled to play at Chicago, and his club ought to see to it that despite his color, he is given every opportunity to show what he can do.(20)

Shippen competed in four more U. S. Open tournaments (1899, 1900,1902, and 1913), but his best finish was in 1902 at Garden City, Long Island, where he again tied for fifth. After serving as club professional at Maidstone for two years, he went to Aronomink Golf Club near Philadelphia. In 1902, he returned to Maidstone and

John Shippen in action. Circa 1913.
(Credit: Bettmann Archives)

served as its professional until 1913. It appears that Shippen, then thirty-four years old and in his prime, was having personal problems. His departure from Maidstone is noted in the club's history with a cryptic statement: "Shippen remained at Maidstone for many years. He was a first class player until the Indians' besetting weakness spoiled his game."(21)

There is some confusion about Shippen's movements over the next few years. From 1913 to 1915, he was a private instructor for a number of wealthy men including steel magnate Henry Clay Frick and ex-New Jersey Governor J. S. Freylinghuysen. At (or about) the same time, he was a professional at Spring Lake Golf & Country Club in New Jersey. From there he served for a season at the Marine and Field Club (later known as the Dyker Beach Club) in Brooklyn, New York. He then returned to Shinnecock Hills as greenkeeper and spent two years there before moving on to the National Golf Links of America (a C.B. Macdonald design right next door) where he was the course maintenance foreman. Within a relatively short time he moved back to Washington, D.C. and took a civil service job in one of the federal public works departments.

By 1921, unwilling and unable to adjust to government employment, he was once again doing what he loved most—playing and teaching golf. Shippen stated that he was the golf instructor at the black-operated Citizens Golf Club in Washington, D. C. from 1921 to 1927, and then spent four years at National Capital Country Club, another golf club owned by African Americans in Laurel, Maryland. Shippen further claimed that he moved to Shady Rest Golf & Country Club, a third black-operated facility, in 1931.(22) Other reports indicate that he became the Shady Rest golf professional as early as 1925, but newspaper accounts during that period tend to support Shippen's chronology.

Unfortunately, he could not have chosen a more untimely moment to take the position of club professional at Shady Rest G&CC. Less than two years had elapsed since the cataclysmic stock market crash of October 1929, and the nation was reeling under the triphammer blows of the Great Depression. During this prolonged economic downturn, expenditures for nonessentials such as country club memberships and golf paraphernalia were among the first to be curtailed or cut from the family budget. More than a few of the wealthy, white-owned country clubs were buffeted in the economic maelstrom, and it was reported that about a quarter of them were forced to close.(23) Shady Rest was particularly vulnerable, serving as it did the economically marginal African American segment of the population. Conventional wisdom would have predicted that Shady Rest would be an early casualty, but conventional wisdom would have been wrong. With shrewd management and good luck, the country club in Scotch Plains managed to survive the worst years of the Depression. But it was difficult.

Shippen (commonly referred to as "Ship") was no less astute in handling his personal finances. To supplement his meager salary, he devised a financial plan for survival that was based on the need to secure additional income. He gave golf lessons, served as caddie master, repaired clubs, sold golf equipment, and gave greenkeeping consultations to nearby golf courses. During good weather, he also had the opportunity to earn extra money in matches that had been arranged by one of his many golf contacts. Though by no means a princely sum, Ship's combined earnings enabled him to satisfy his basic needs. Moreover, having negotiated living accommodations in the Shady Rest clubhouse as a condition of employment, Shippen's overhead expenses were relatively small, thereby adding to his disposable income.(24)

John Shippen was a private, complex person who preferred to go his own way. In 1898, when his father completed his tenure as pastor on the Shinnecock Indian Reservation and returned to Washington, D. C., every family member except John Junior went with him. Not long after his family's departure, Shippen married a Shinnecock woman named Effie Walker. Sadly, they were only married a short time before Effie died. The circumstances of her death are not known, but it would not be unreasonable to assume that her death was traumatic for her young husband. Indeed, one wonders if her death precipitated the previously mentioned problem he may have had with alcohol. On May 27, 1901, he married a second Shinnecock woman, Maude Elliot Lee. Out of that union, six children were born within a nine-year span.

For more than a quarter of a century, John Shippen lived primarily within the insular world of white golf, while his family lived on the reservation. He also changed locations fairly frequently, leading one to speculate about the reasons. Was it because he encountered racism? Was it because of his drinking? Or was it a combination of both? From all indications, Maude shouldered the bulk of the family responsibilities because Shippen failed to provide for their needs with any degree of consistency. As he grew further and further apart from his family, he and Maude eventually separated.(25) Although their relationship became increasingly strained, Shippen heeded his wife's advice to move to Washington, D.C. After his brief sojourn in the civil service, he entered a world that was new for him—the world of African American golf. He would remain there for the rest of his life.

Shippen's relationships with the black residents of Scotch Plains were tentative and problematic. Some found fault with his style of instruction while others thought he was aloof. Whether any of this bothered him is uncertain. What *is* known is that he was fond of hot dogs and Milky Way bars, and that he had a small circle of friends who respected his ability and integrity. Always eager to be in their company, he frequently joined them for a trip to the movies or a card-playing session. Since he was not a churchgoer, he did not endear himself to some members of the cliquish black community. On the golf course he was serious and thoroughly professional, but he was also known to go on occasional quiet drinking benders. It's uncertain whether he attended his wife's funeral in 1957, but there was a degree of reconciliation with some of his children in the later years of his life.

After an episode of kidney disease in 1960, Shippen recovered sufficiently to continue to play golf well into his eighties. His downfall at the Open in 1896 remained etched indelibly in his consciousness, and he usually spoke about it when he reminisced. John Shippen had come from a family of middle-class, well-educated, high-achieving African Americans, and he had been a bit of a misfit—a fact that was probably a source of mutual disappointment. The 1969 *Tuesday* magazine article included something he once said: ". . . I wonder if I did the right thing when I quit school and went into golf. Maybe I should have kept going and gone to Yale like my brother who's a teacher." Almost in the same breath, he concluded: "I wonder until I look out the window and see that golf course. Then I realize how much enjoyment I've gotten out of the game, and I don't wonder any more."

After his days at Shady Rest were over, Shippen lived near the golf course with friends until he was unable to care for himself. One of his daughters moved him to a nursing home in Newark, New Jersey. There, on July 15, 1968, John Matthew Shippen, Jr., the first golf professional to be born in the United States of America, and the first African American to play in the U.S. Open, died peacefully.

In 1990, prompted by a newspaper article about Shippen's life that had appeared in a Newark newspaper, a small group of townspeople from Scotch Plains and nearby communities came together to explore the possibility of developing a project to honor his memory. After a few meetings, the John Shippen African American Commemorative Committee was formed. The following year, thanks to a modest contribution provided by the Merck Pharmaceutical Company, the Committee sponsored its first golf tournament with the proceeds used to provide a scholarship to a deserving minority high school athlete.

Thurman Simmons (left) and Hanno Shippen Smith (right) at the John M. Shippen gravesite. Simmons is president of the John Shippen Memorial Foundation, Inc., and Smith is John Shippen's grandson.   (Credit: Mr. Hanno Shippen Smith)

Annual tournaments have been held each year since, with subsequent scholarships awarded to minority high school students for academic achievement. In 1993 the Committee bought a headstone for John Shippen's grave at the Rosedale Cemetery in Linden, New Jersey. In 1995, now established as a not-for-profit, tax-exempt organization, the Committee was reorganized as the John Shippen Memorial Golf Foundation, Inc.(26)

Joseph Bartholomew

"There's no such thing as 'get rich quick.' Take your time. Be honest, listen, and learn." This quote, which appeared in a November, 1949 *Fortune* magazine interview, offers words of counsel from

Joseph Manual Bartholomew, Sr. to young African Americans. In his day, Joe Bartholomew—one of the wealthiest black men in the city of New Orleans—was an unlikely American success story.

Bartholomew was born in New Orleans on August 1, 1881.(27) He went as far as the eighth grade before striking out on his own at the age of twelve. In his first job, working for a white family, he was expected to arrive at the house of his employer well before dawn to clean the pantry. After he learned the routine, Joe was usually able to complete his chores by early afternoon. Not one to idle away his free time, he soon began using the remaining daylight hours to caddie at nearby Audubon Golf Course. He taught himself to play and soon became good enough to teach others. Demonstrating an additional talent for course maintenance, he was placed in charge of the greens.

No longer in school nor employed elsewhere, young Bartholomew could now devote all of his time to golf. As time passed, his playing improved to the extent that whenever someone with a fancy golf reputation arrived, arrangements would be made to pit the newcomer against him. Joe was always the winner. On one memorable occasion, he toured Audubon in an amazing 62 strokes. Among the many opponents he faced were golfing greats Walter Hagen and Gene Sarazen.

After Scotsman Freddie McLeod won the 1908 U. S. Open, he accepted the job as Audubon's club professional. Before long, he and Bartholomew were engaged in a series of head-to-head matches. "I beat Mr. McLeod [sometimes] and he beat me [other times]," Joe recalled. McLeod was so impressed with Bartholomew's ability that he soon hired him as his assistant.

While working for McLeod, Joe learned the art of clubmaking. In one year alone, thanks to his newly acquired ability, he earned nearly $10,000 for replacing equipment that had been destroyed in a clubhouse fire. In addition to playing, teaching, and clubmaking, Bartholomew's affinity for greenkeeping and course maintenance led him into landscaping. Barely forty years old, Bartholomew had mastered a wide range of golf-related skills, and had developed a reputation for his many talents.

In 1922, when officials of Metarie Golf Club on the outskirts of New Orleans decided to build a new 18-hole course, they turned to Joe Bartholomew to undertake the project. H. T. Cottam, a wealthy

New Orleans businessman, was a club member who had confidence in Joe's ability to handle the assignment.(28) It was Cottam who persuaded other members to send Bartholomew to Long Island, New York, for further training and experience. While there, Joe was fortunate to work with Seth Raynor, the noted golf course architect. Under Raynor's tutelage, Bartholomew learned the intricacies of building greens, shaping fairways, and molding bunkers. With his innate imagination and his newly acquired knowledge, Joe constructed small-scale Plasticine models for later use in the design of the Metarie course.

The site chosen for the new course was untouched wilderness, and some expressed doubt that anyone could gain *access* to the area— much less clear it for use as a golf course. Undismayed by the naysayers, the intrepid Bartholomew began to clear the land (frequently working at night to avoid the inquisitive eyes of potential competitors). After several months and the outlay of a considerable amount of money, some of the club members began to grow uneasy about the pace of Bartholomew's progress. At the urging of an especially anxious member, Bartholomew was summoned to a meeting where he was grilled about what was taking place. Eventually, the group asked to be taken to the site. Because it was inaccessible by automobile, Joe made special arrangements for the members to be transported by horse-drawn wagon the next day. When they arrived, they were surprised to see what Joe had quietly accomplished. They were particularly impressed by the greens. Drawing on what he'd learned on Long Island, Joe had fashioned greens that were elevated 10 to 12 inches above the surrounding turf. This design resulted in excellent drainage, a feature for which he was highly praised. In fact, Bartholomew's severest critic the night before was so pleased that he recommended an increase in Joe's salary.(29)

Joe remained at the new Metarie course for a few years after it opened—teaching, making clubs, and giving advice. Yet, despite his contributions to the club's success, simply because of his skin color, Bartholomew was not allowed to play even a single round on the course he had built.

From Metarie, Bartholomew moved to New Orleans Country Club to work as the greenkeeper. He was there only briefly before he was appointed to build what is now the City Park No.1 course in

New Orleans. By this time he was recognized as one of the area's leading golf course architects. Over the next eight years, he built the City Park No. 2 course and the Pontchartrain Park course. According to all accounts, Bartholomew neither sought nor received any compensation for building the three New Orleans courses.

During this same period, Bartholomew built courses in the cities of Hammond, Covington, Abita, Algiers Springs, Slidell, and Baton Rouge, and one in the adjoining state of Mississippi. In each instance, however, it was a repeat of the absurd and demeaning Metarie experience. He could *build* the course, but he couldn't *play* it. Finally fed up with the prejudice that was preventing African Americans from playing the game, Bartholomew constructed a seven-hole course for black golfers on property he owned in nearby Harahan, Louisiana. It was separate, but—even with his superb skills—he could not make it equal.

In the mid-1930s, with the experience, contacts, and resources he had acquired from his years in golf course construction, Bartholomew established a general construction company and began to diversify his activities. In 1934, he received a major contract from the city of New Orleans to repave Tulane Avenue, an important commercial artery. During World War II his construction company worked for one of the large shipbuilders in the city; after the war it was involved in erecting foundations for numerous factories, office buildings, and housing complexes. With profits earned from the construction business, Bartholomew invested in an insurance company, established an ice cream manufacturing plant,and entered into a number of lucrative real estate ventures. It is no surprise that Joe Bartholomew was regarded by many in the white business community as someone with an inborn talent for making money.

A modest, mild-mannered man, Bartholomew was a devout Catholic who made substantial financial contributions to the predominantly black Xavier and Dillard Universities in New Orleans. He seldom mentioned his personal achievements, preferring to let them speak for themselves. One of his few social outlets was membership in the Original Illinois Carnival Club, organized by a group of prominent African American men primarily for the purpose of participating in the annual Mardi Gras festivities. He continued to play golf into his eighties, stopping only in the last two years of his life when his health began to fail. He died at home on October 12, 1971, and is buried in St. Mary's Cemetery in New Orleans.

In recognition of his achievements in the field of athletics, Bartholomew was inducted into the Greater New Orleans Sports Hall of Fame on February 4, 1972. He was the first African American to be so honored.(30) On July 2, 1979, more than two decades after it originally opened as a nine-hole segregated facility, the newly renovated Pontchartrain Golf Course was officially renamed the

Joseph Bartholomew, golf course builder, relaxing at the Pontchartrain Golf Course in New Orleans during the 1960s.   (Credit: Mrs. Ruth Creech)

Joseph M. Bartholomew, Sr. Municipal Golf Course. In his remarks at the dedication ceremony, Mayor Ernest N. Morial pointedly noted that during the years when Joe Bartholomew built many of the golf courses in the New Orleans area, he could not receive permission to play on those same courses.

Dewey Brown

Born September 21, 1898, on a small farm in rural North Carolina, Dewey Brown moved to New Jersey with his family when he was a young boy. By the age of eight, he was caddying at Madison Golf Club. He also earned money as a member of the groundskeeping crew. It was not uncommon for him to work 10-hour stretches cutting fairways behind a horse-drawn mower for a dollar a day.(31)

As he grew older, Dewey's skills as a caddie and a golfer improved steadily. By 1916, he had also developed an interest in fashioning golf clubs and soon began working under Tom Hucknell at Morris County (New Jersey) Country Club. Hucknell, a respected clubmaker, saw promise in the young man and started teaching him the finer points of the craft. Brown learned quickly. He made a set of hickory-shafted clubs for Charles "Chick" Evans, Jr., which Evans used in winning the 1916 U.S. Amateur Championship. Later on, Brown's expertise as a clubmaker would command the respect and praise of other notable golfers.

In addition to his skill at making and repairing clubs, Brown's aptitude for teaching did not go unnoticed. Before the age of twenty, he left Morris County Country Club to join the renowned Willie Norton at Shawnee-on-the-Delaware in eastern Pennsylvania. While there, Dewey began giving golf lessons as part of his duties as Norton's assistant. When Shawnee closed at the end of the season, Dewey would go to work for another well-known clubmaker, George Lowe, at the famous Baltusrol Golf Club in Springfield, New Jersey. In the spring, Brown would return to Shawnee for the new season.

As a bona fide golf professional, Brown played in a number of local tournaments. With a wife and three young sons to support, Brown eventually left Shawnee and bought a small farm in Newton,

Professional golfer Dewey Brown, at
Shawnee-on-the-Delaware in the early 1930s.
(Credit: Mr. Roland Brown)

New Jersey. Later, he opened a modest restaurant and catering business in Dover, New Jersey. Golf, however, was always his mainstay. He served for a short time at Hollywood Golf Club in Deal, New Jersey, and then moved on to Fennimore Golf Club in White Plains, New York. In 1925, Dewey returned to Shawnee and rejoined Willie Norton. He remained there for the next 12 years.

During his lifetime, Brown taught golf and made clubs for a number of the nation's leading businessmen, professionals, and statesmen. Among those who purchased his clubs were President Warren G. Harding and Charles Dawes, vice president under Calvin

Coolidge. Brown received letters from both men stating that he had done "an outstanding job."

In 1928, Dewey Brown became the first African American member of the Professional Golfer's Association (PGA). Since Brown had very light skin, later events would suggest that the PGA was unaware of his racial identity when he was granted membership. There's no evidence that Brown deliberately misrepresented himself to the organization. Apparently, he simply did not raise the issue.

Brown's stature as a golfer and clubmaker continued to grow during the next few years but he also had an unexpected setback. In 1934, without any explanation or forewarning, the PGA withdrew his eligibility. To this day—even though they are unable to substantiate their suspicions with irrefutable evidence—Brown family members remain convinced that someone informed PGA officials of Dewey Brown's African ancestry, and that was the reason for his expulsion.(32)

Disappointed but not embittered, he left Shawnee to try his hand at golf club management and administration. He gained experience in these two capacities at Rockaway River Country Club in Denville, New Jersey and at Knoll Golf Club in Boonton, New Jersey. In 1946, he was persuaded to return to Shawnee for a third time. The well-known choral director Fred Waring had recently purchased the establishment and needed someone to manage it. Dewey Brown was his choice, and the entertainer spared no efforts to recruit him.

On this occasion, however, Brown's stay at Shawnee was short-lived. In 1947, he bought the historic Cedar River House and Golf Club at Indian Lake, New York, in the Adirondack mountains. The nine-hole, 2,720-yard course was his prized possession. In addition to owning it, he served as the club professional for the next 26 years. Eleven years after buying the Cedar River club, Brown became a member of the Golf Course Superintendents Association of America. Indicative of the respect he commanded, on at least one occasion he was selected to represent the northeastern chapter at the organization's annual convention. In the early 1960s, at the insistence and encouragement of his many friends and golf associates in the northeast, Brown applied for reinstatement in the PGA. Two years later— more than 30 years after he'd been dropped from the rolls without one word of explanation—Dewey Brown was formally "re-elected to class 'A' membership" in the PGA.

During his illustrious career in golf, the smooth-swinging, dapper, and gentlemanly Dewey Brown was affiliated with more than a dozen of the better-known private golf clubs in the New Jersey, New York, and Pennsylvania area. He had four holes-in-one, and he played golf with such notables as dancer/actor Fred Astaire, baseball player Jimmie Foxx, and choral director Fred Waring. In his capacity as golf professional and club manager, Brown met scores of prominent people. Among his many acquaintances were Bing Crosby, J. P. Morgan, Al Jolson, Bob Hope, and Walter Hagen. It is quite possible that he and John Shippen knew each other because they both lived in central New Jersey at the same time. On at least one occasion Brown played a match at Shady Rest Golf & Country Club while Shippen was the club professional.

Enormously proud of his three sons, all of whom were fine golfers, Brown once drove some 300 miles through the night from his home in Dover, New Jersey, to Lake Placid, New York, to walk beside his son Roland and watch him win the Kate Smith amateur golf tournament at Craig Wood Golf Course.

In 1972, members of the Cedar River Club and community officials honored Brown's achievements with a surprise banquet and town celebration. The following year, on December 23, 1973, Dewey Brown died peacefully in Newton, New Jersey. Fittingly, he was buried in the Indian Lake Cemetery across the road from his beloved Cedar River Golf Club.

It comes as no surprise that noted golf writer Herb Graffis referred to Dewey Brown as one of golf's "pioneer personalities."(33)

Five Lives in Retrospect

Viewed collectively *and* separately, the lives of these five men reveal an interesting assortment of similarities and differences. All were of African ancestry and suffered because of racial discrimination; all were born into meager circumstances; all loved the game of golf; all were quiet and unassuming; and all enjoyed the respect and admiration of their colleagues. In addition—with the possible exception of

Grant, whose level of play is not a matter of record—all were top-notch golfers. Shippen, Bartholomew, and Brown caddied in their youth and it is likely that Speedy did also. Grant, on the other hand, lived outside the orbit of golf in his youth, so it is unlikely that he ever carried someone's bag for money.

None of these remarkable men had ostentatious lifestyles, although, in their later years, Bartholomew became quite well-off, and Grant had a comfortable existence. Of the group, Shippen probably lived most frugally and seems to be the only one who had a distant relationship with his family. Speedy was the only one who moved almost exclusively within African American circles throughout his entire life. While Grant played golf with his black friends, he had many white patients in his large dental practice and he was a member of the almost all-white Harvard dental faculty.

Each of these men made sizeable contributions to the game, and have earned a well-deserved place in contemporary African American golf history.

3 | Humpin' Bags— The Black Caddie

When New Year's Day of 1900 dawned on the nation, the plight of African Americans was largely unchanged from the situation that prevailed immediately after the Civil War. The all-too-familiar problems of poverty, unemployment, inadequate housing, and a myriad of other social ills continued to beset black Americans. In such an environment, which was further aggravated by severe limitations of access, the number of black golfers remained pitifully small. It borders on the miraculous that a few were able to find the money, the time and a place to play.

Somewhat paradoxically, however, there was a small group of black golfers who played fairly regularly and whose numbers were growing. They were the country club caddies and, to a lesser degree, other black club employees. For the most part, they lived in the South and were both literally and metaphorically the backbone of early twentieth century golf in the United States.

Photographs of black caddies taken during those early days suggest that many of them could not have been more than eight or nine years old. It was an era when flagrant abuses of child labor were widespread. Young souls labored from 14 to 16 hours a day, six days a week for a pittance. Working conditions in the mills and coal mines were so hazardous that many children were severely injured or even killed in work-related accidents.(1) But in the perverse logic of racial segregation, black youth, especially those in the South, were not allowed to work in the mills, and few were given the "opportunity" to toil in the coal mines of West Virginia or the glass foundries of Ten-

John D. Rockefeller posing with caddies in Ormond Beach, Florida. Circa 1920s.

nessee. This was a major reason why young African Americans of that generation worked as caddies in such disproportionate numbers. In the mind of the average white country club official, caddies were simply another segment of the black servant class who did not have a significant role to play in the nation's growth.

Another unfortunate belief, held even by those with a fair degree of social enlightenment, was the misconception that the caddie pursued his activities in much the same sort of idyllic natural surroundings as the farmer who was engaged in wholesome outdoor work. Consequently, when the crusade against child labor began to take hold, the young black caddie was overlooked, even though his working conditions often were as exploitive as those of his white counterparts in the industrial sector.

Ill-fed, ill-clad, and often barefoot, the black caddie appeared at the caddie shed shortly after dawn and remained on the course until late in the day. More often than not, he was required to travel considerable distances to and from the course.(2) Few of them went beyond elementary school, with the majority not completing more than the first three or four years. Their meals, eaten haphazardly, were of questionable nutritional value, and because the courses were often located far from neighborhood shopping areas, young caddies frequently were overcharged by nearby food vendors. During inclement weather the youngsters had to seek shelter in the caddie shed. It was usually poorly lit, poorly ventilated, and poorly heated— an uncomfortable place to be in the chilly months of early spring and late fall. Constantly exposed to these conditions, the caddies were particularly vulnerable to a variety of respiratory ailments.

In his eagerness to earn as much as possible, a caddie often walked the full 18 holes three times in a single summer day, sometimes "carrying double" (two bags). This could mean walking as much as 12 to 15 miles, shouldering golf bags that might weigh from 20 to 50 pounds each. On a flat course in cool weather, the level of physical exertion would be bad enough. But on a hilly course under a broiling summer sun, the caddie was exposed to the perils of fatigue and heat exhaustion. At the end of the round, the caddie was also expected to clean the owner's clubs and deposit them at a designated location.

In addition, it was not unusual for the caddie to turn over a por-

One of the earliest known photographs of the Augusta National Golf Club caddies. Circa 1935. Note the number of clubs in the bag on the left. (Credit: Frank Christian)

tion of his earnings to the caddiemaster at the end of a round or at the end of the day. The caddiemaster made the assignments, and a young caddie soon learned that he would have to satisfy the financial demands of the caddiemaster if he expected to earn an adequate income. He also learned that by becoming especially proficient at his job he quite possibly could become the favorite of a member who was a good tipper, a good golfer or, preferably, both. By caddying regularly for one or more such members, he might also achieve a certain amount of independence from the whims or outright tyranny of the caddiemaster.

Due to a variety of reasons, however, even the most popular caddies were not working every hour of the day, every day of the week. There were long stretches of idleness that varied with the time of day, weather, season, and day of the week. To a lesser degree, these periods were also affected by events at the home club or at nearby clubs. The golfing-ambitious caddie often used this "downtime" to hone his playing skills, especially his short game. He might spend hours practicing "touch" shots with the short irons. At many courses, caddies were able to fashion a practice "green" which might be nothing more than a patch of bare ground. Nevertheless, the improvised putting surface provided something of an opportunity to judge speed, slope, and distance. Sometimes, at the end of the day, a caddie would sneak in a short session of bunker play or other trouble shots. All of this prepared him for his weekly competition.

Once a week, usually Monday mornings, a large number of private clubs allowed employees to play the course. Those were the occasions when caddies, most likely playing with incomplete sets of hand-me-down clubs, took on their peers with an intensity and daring that rivaled that of the top amateurs and many of the professionals. It was not uncommon for the best-playing caddies to shoot sub-par rounds during these Monday matches—some even set course records.(3) At times, club members placed bets on the outcomes. The wagering among the caddies themselves could be fast and furious as well. Of course teasing, swearwords, and colorful speech were the order of the day.

Out of the caddie ranks emerged some of the finest golfers the country has ever seen. The golfing exploits of such ex-caddies as Gene Sarazen, Walter Hagen, Sam Snead, Ben Hogan, and Byron Nelson are well known. Less known are the caddying careers of black golfers Charlie Sifford, Ted Rhodes, and Lee Elder. Clyde Martin was another one of those highly-rated—but seldom mentioned—black golfers who began his career as a caddie. Born in southern Maryland, he began to caddie at the Congressional Country Club in Bethesda, Maryland in his pre-teen years. This was the period in the late 1920s when the renowned Tommy Armour held sway as the club's professional. Armour soon recognized Martin's golfing talents and before long he began to pit the young caddie against visitors looking for (betting) "action." Martin rarely lost in those head-to-head matches but, following the "rules" of the day, he was never given the opportunity to play in national competition.

By 1939, however, his playing abilities were so well known in black golf circles that he was named as the club professional at the newly-opened (and segregated) Langston Golf Course in Washington D.C. In less than 18 months after the Langston appointment, world heavy-weight boxing champion Joe Louis hired Martin as his personal coach. Martin remained with Louis until 1942 when Louis went into the army. After the war, Martin played fairly regularly on the black golf circuit until his premature death in the early 1950s.

Virtually unknown to the golfing world are the deeds of a black golfer and caddie who was mentioned in a 1938 issue of United Golfer and Other Sports. This somewhat poorly edited magazine, no longer in print, was published monthly by the Fairview Golf Club in Philadelphia and contained a variety of sports and general interest items, with golf featured prominently. Two articles appeared in a 1938 issue describing the golfing abilities of a caddie in superlatives comparable to those that have been written about today's golfing sensation, Tiger Woods. The first article was a copy of a letter dated July 9, 1938. It was sent by Joseph Lavitt to the editor, Joseph H. Hudson.

Dear Sir:

In answer to yours of the 30th June, J. C. Hamilton is all that is claimed for him and if anything I think with continuous playing he could beat the best golfers in the world on any golf course you could name.

Without doubt he is the longest driver in the world and his short game is not far behind.

Enclosed is an unsolicited newspaper article which will explain itself and in addition to this J. C. was asked to come down to the Norwich Country Club and exhibit for some of the staff of "Life" magazine. He accepted and promptly proceeded to outdo himself by driving a ball from the 18th tee to the green, a distance of 353 yards, of which 340 was on the fly.

To drive [a] 300-yard green is child's play for him and to make 500-yard greens in two is also a cinch.

His full name and address is James C. Hamilton, Bradenton, Florida . . .

Especially significant was the short final paragraph of Lavitt's letter:

I had him entered in the U. S. Open and due to him being a Negro my application and fee was returned.

Although the exact source of the second article in the same issue of the publication is not identified, it well might have been the "unsolicited newspaper article" mentioned in Lavitt's letter. The towns that are mentioned suggest that the locale was either in the southern Maryland/northern Virginia area or in southern New England. The article reveals that Hamilton was in his early twenties, stood about five feet ten inches tall, and weighed about 165 pounds. When he was younger, Hamilton caddied for baseball pitcher "Dizzy" Dean when Dean was in Florida for spring training. Lavitt, who was the owner of a grain company in the town of Rockville, persuaded Hamilton to travel north to work for him

Shortly after Hamilton arrived from Florida, the writer of the article was invited to observe the former caddie in action. The person who extended the invitation (probably Lavitt) stated that Hamilton could " . . . hit 'em as far as any golfer I ever saw, and I have seen all of them these years I have been going to Florida." Despite these claims, the writer was unconvinced until he followed the "colored boy" on a round at the Manchester Golf Course. In short order, the skeptic joined the ranks of the believers. "His prize feat that day," wrote the new convert, "was driving the 10th green which is a few yards over 300 and with a slight rise before the green. Here 'J. C.' lashed into one and the ball soared to come to rest about eight feet from the pin." Overwhelmed by what he had seen, the writer continued to praise him effusively:

But even the tee shots I saw him hit out there left me unconvinced that he could give Jimmy Thompson a real battle in long distance hitting.

It was wiser, I felt, to wait until some- one better qualified than I could put an official stamp of approval on this transplanted southern caddy (sic).

This morning I got this official stamp of approval.

It came from Barney Gunshinan, professional at the Norwich Golf Club where "J. C." played a round Friday afternoon.

Barney raved about him over the phone this morning. 'He's as long a hitter as I have ever seen,' he said, 'and I have seen

Jimmy Thompson. I never happened to get a chance to watch Sammy Snead but I'll back this kid against anyone I have ever seen hit. He sure can smack 'em.'

Barney stopped for breath and went on. 'You know our first hole—it is 327 yards. Well, this kid drove that green twice. The first time he carried the green and was about five feet past the cup. That is a real smack . . .

'All the way around,' Barney continued, this boy was hitting terrific drives. You know our 16th hole? Well, it is 559 yards. J. C. cut the corner here and with his second shot was six feet from the cup. I need a brassie and an approach shot to get home there after my tee shot. The interesting thing about this boy making it in two was that his second had to be hit out of a cuppy lie.

J. C.'s whole game is good. The day I had the first viewing of him over at Manchester he was putting badly being unused to the greens, but he was even par when I left . . .

On a recent Sunday, Rockville's new and long-hitting citizen invaded Franconia at Springfield and scores of golfers halted play to watch him . . . (4)

The writer was even more amazed when he learned that until three weeks earlier, J.C had never owned a complete set of clubs. It was then that Lavitt, realizing the golfing potential of his new employee, bought J.C a new bag and a new set of clubs. And all of J.C.'s feats were ac-complished long before the advent of high compression balls, graphite shafts, and woods made with space-age metals.

There was a fleeting mention of J.C. in the July 25, 1942, issue of the Chicago Defender *in which he was referred to as "George Hamilton [of] Bradentown (sic) Fla., thought by many observers to be the longest driver in American golf." Nothing further is known about Hamilton's subse-quent career. Like so many other talented African American golfers, he simply disappeared into golfing oblivion. If* United Golfer and Other Sports *had not existed, the little that is known about J. C. Hamilton's re-markable golfing achievements never would have surfaced.*

It makes one wonder if there were other "J.C. Hamiltons" over the years . . . who never received any attention.

The longer he worked at it, the more knowledgeable the young caddie became about the game, the course, and the people whose bags he carried. Besides improving his ability to follow the flight of the ball, the maturing caddie developed a keen sense of distance. "How far?" was the most frequent question asked of him by the golfers, and he had to be able to reckon distances accurately from any spot on the course. He also had to be thoroughly familiar with local hazards, the texture of the grass on the greens, the "feel" of the sand in the bunkers, the places where the wind swirled, and the dangers that lurked behind and alongside the greens. Although he could not make a ruling, the caddie had to have more than a nodding acquaintance with the rules of the game. An understanding of, and appreciation for, proper golf etiquette was important as well. Perhaps the greatest asset to the aspiring caddie lay in his capacity to assess the physical and mental qualities of the person for whom he was caddying. One writer summed it up admirably when he remarked:

"Caddying . . . is a lot more than lugging a heavy bag of clubs. The caddy is an amateur meteorologist and psychologist, an authority on his own course with a knowledge of the rules of the game. He is the player's helper, rooter and coach, [and in championship golf] his bodyguard and protector from the crowd, his toughest critic and his best friend."(5)

While the caddie had to deal with the psychological problems of the golfer, he also had to handle his own personal problems. During the long hours of idleness, caddies frequently developed lifestyles that were detrimental to their well-being. They often smoked heavily, abused alcohol, and gambled. Some neglected their families and their own health care. Yet there were others who were responsible and respected members of their communities. Often deeply religious, they foreswore the vices, lived frugally, and used their meager earnings to sustain a cohesive household. Because most of them had failed to complete their education, these men of integrity did their utmost to ensure the education of their children.

Of all the indignities endured by African American service employees, none is more bitterly resented than being treated as a nonperson. Things were said or done in their presence as if they did not exist. Generations of black servants, bellhops, waitresses, and Pullman car porters knew they had to accept this denial of their humanity if they wanted to keep their jobs. Before World War II, for example, it was not unusual for a golfing publication to contain a photograph of a group of white golfers with their black caddies. In the accompanying caption, the golfers are usually identified by name but the caddies are not.

An even more dramatic demonstration of this kind of callous insensitivity was described by syndicated columnist Dewayne Wickham in a gripping account of his life as a black orphan living in the Cherry Hill ghetto of Baltimore. Desperately needing a job, the preadolescent Wickham obtained employment as a caddie at one of the all-white country clubs on the outskirts of the city. One day while caddying for two female club members, he overheard one of them tell the other of an extramarital affair she was having with one of the male club members. She described her activities in intimate detail without the slightest regard for his presence. Young Dewayne was not trying to eavesdrop; the woman merely carried on her conversation without any attempt to lower her voice. But that was not the end of the incident. Wickham was totally unprepared for what happened a few moments later:

> "As we walked away from her playing partner, the woman looked over her shoulder several times as though to measure the separation. Then, when the spacing was just right, she farted. The sound was unmistakable, a staccato eruption of body gas. She didn't look at me and she didn't offer a word of apology. And why should she? By now it was all too clear to me that I didn't matter. My being around hadn't mattered when she shared her adulterous secrets. And it surely didn't matter when she had to fart. I was the 'Invisible Man' Ralph Ellison had written about in 1952—one of those black men white people so often don't see not because we're hidden from their view, but because they choose not to acknowledge our presence." (6)

Wherever they gather, caddies of bygone years—both black and white—tell similar variations of Wickham's experiences. One of the big differences between black and white caddies in those days was the fact that whites did not have to accept this treatment for long. Simply because of their skin color, they had more opportunities to find other work; blacks had to put up with it. Many—even today—have never forgiven those who treated them as inanimate objects. In spite of the indignities, these proud men were an integral part of golf's rich tapestry. If there is any doubt, a recent episode should set the record straight.

On Monday morning, April 10, 1995, the sports pages of newspapers across the United States and some foreign countries carried the story of American golfer Ben Crenshaw's victory in the Masters Tournament at the Augusta National Golf Club in Augusta, Georgia. In most cases, the written account was accompanied by a photograph of Crenshaw and his African American caddie, Carl Jackson, taken moments after Crenshaw sank the winning putt. For four grueling days, these two men had worried, plotted, prayed, and labored to overcome the challenges of the unforgiving and deceptively treacherous Augusta course. Captured in the pictorial tableau is the story worth the proverbial million words. Two men—one black, one white—bonded by a common experience, joyful yet humbled by the glory of the moment. The diminutive Crenshaw, emotionally drained and in tears, is being supported and embraced by the larger, comforting frame of Jackson. The ordeal was over and now they could release the enormous tension that had accumulated since the opening day of the tournament.

But there were other aspects of the photograph that relate to issues much broader and deeper than a sporting victory. They deal with a nation's tortured past that is enmeshed in the twisted contradictions of injustice, benevolence, loyalty, hatred, trust, and fear. For that brief moment, though, the two men had transcended the past and had come to terms with a shared humanity based on interdependence, talent, mutual respect, confidence, and determination. To be sure, financial considerations were important to both. But they were neither the sole nor the overriding concern. In many ways, that photograph is not only a window into the lives of many generations of black caddies but a vindication of their perception of self-esteem as well, regardless of how others might try to make them invisible.

On any given day, unless the weather is exceptionally grim, former caddies can be found clustered in small groups in or near a golf course clubhouse. The scene is almost identical whether they gather at Rogers Park Golf Course in Tampa, Florida, at Langston Golf Course in Washington, D. C., or at Palmer Park Golf Course in Detroit, Michigan. They are the last of a fast-fading generation of black caddies who have been retired by age, infirmity, the motorized golf cart, or some combination of the three.

With colorful nicknames such as "Killer," "Lips," and "Cut Shot," they begin to arrive after the heavy morning road traffic has subsided. Many eat breakfast and their midday meal at the golf course. The meals are not large in bulk, but because of their high fat and sugar content, they are loaded with calories. The clothes of some are out of fashion and frayed, and their speech is laced with wit, sarcasm, and expletives. Many smoke heavily with a casual disregard for the opinions or sensibilities of others. Some are also without the benefit of health or retirement insurance, and they frequently live on their Social Security benefits that may be supplemented by support from family members. It would be wrong, however, to believe that they lead lives of unrelieved misery. With few traces of bitterness, they prefer to recall the acts of kindness shown to them by the golfing public (sometimes even to their families) rather than dwell on the ugliness and hardships of the past.

Many of these elderly black men no longer have a spring in their step; it disappeared over the years as they trudged down untold fairways with large golf bags on their shoulders. In the course of their careers, some caddies have even had to undergo scrutiny by Secret Service officials (President Dwight Eisenhower was a member of Augusta National), endure repeated questions from the media, withstand tasteless intrusions by autograph seekers, and listen to bigoted comments from members of a gallery. Yet, a gleam comes into their eyes as they recall the excitement of a long-forgotten match or the shotmaking of a particularly gifted player.

The caddie who carried for a player in a modern major tournament had to make detailed preparations for such an event. He arrived at the course at dawn's first light to pace off distances and to make sure that bags contained no more than the allowed 14 clubs. An up-to-date yardage book, an umbrella, and an ample supply of balls and towels were important "musts." During inclement weather,

Ben Crenshaw gets a hug from his caddie, Carl Jackson, on the 18ᵗʰ green after winning the 1995 Masters. (Credit: AP/World Wide Photo)

it might be necessary to add rain gear, an extra sweater, and winter gloves. The caddie might also carry assorted items such as adhesive tape, resin, talcum powder, candy bars, fruit, chewing gum, and cigarettes. It is easy to see how the load could exceed 40 pounds.

Veteran caddies are proud men who firmly believe that theirs was "a very respectable profession." After a lifetime of observing presidents, royalty, celebrities, congressmen, business tycoons, and members of the clergy, many are often shrewd judges of the human condition. Few things escape their eyes and ears, and they have the memories of elephants. Whether it is Greg Norman's misfortune on the last day of the 1996 Masters or some unknown golfer's failure to sink an 18-inch putt on the final green, the grizzled caddie is convinced that "everybody has a choke [level]."(7)

That pithy observation aptly reveals an acute appreciation of human frailty under duress. In such situations, an experienced caddie knew that he had to be a steadying influence on his golfer and get him or her back on track. Before the recent emergence of the consulting sports psychologist, the caddie often filled that role using a variety of techniques (today it's called "behavior modification") learned not from theory but from years of experience and shared knowledge passed by word of mouth from one caddie to the next.

Unfortunately, less than 10 years after the end of World War II, signs began to appear that the caddie ranks were shrinking. A variety of attempts were made to stem the decline. Caddies were offered more money, caddie shacks were renovated and equipped with more amenities, and parking facilities and recreational games were provided. Caddiemasters visited local high schools to recruit students for summer employment. A number of college financial assistance programs for caddies with good scholastic records (the Evans Scholarship, for example) were launched with great expectations. Despite these efforts, the number of caddies nationwide has steadily decreased and, for all intents and purposes, caddies are now an "endangered species." Many of the remaining black country club caddies see themselves as a dying breed and openly predict that they will cease to exist by the year 2010. They also predict that the number of black caddies on the major tours will continue to decline.(8)

Why has this happened? First and foremost was the arrival of the motorized golf cart on the national scene, followed closely by the installation of concrete paths to accommodate the carts. For older golfers and those less inclined to walking, a motorized cart was an appealing way to get through 18 holes of golf. Furthermore, the cost of renting a cart, when shared by two players, was usually cheaper for each player than the use of a caddie. In recent years, college graduates and family members of touring professionals have chosen to caddie as a way of making a living. These new caddies, although relatively few in number, have had an adverse impact on the earnings of some club caddies.

Another blow to caddiedom came when the PGA Tour permitted professional golfers to use their own caddies instead of the caddies at the club where an event was being held. This effectively erased yet another major source of income for the club caddie. When, in 1983, Augusta National Golf Club revoked a long-cherished rule prohibiting professional golfers from using caddies from outside the club pool, it was tantamount to the last straw. As one journalist observed, "It changed the look of the Masters forever. No longer was each player flanked by a black man in a white jumpsuit, both of them framed by emerald green . . . " He commented further: " . . . In emotional terms, being muscled out of the Masters was a blow to their self worth and dignity."(9)

Rightly or wrongly, Augusta's caddies felt their situation was unique and deserved special consideration. In contrast to other country club caddies who have accepted their fate with resignation, the Augusta National caddies who were affected by the 1983 decision are a small group of disillusioned, disgruntled, and unforgiving men. More than a decade later, their wounds are unhealed.

Despite the many incentives that are offered, it is particularly difficult to interest black youth in caddying. One major deterrent is the subservient, "Uncle Tom" image of the caddie in the minds of the younger generation of African Americans. Moreover, caddying is a strenuous affair, done at times in uncomfortable weather and for long hours without particularly attractive incomes. Even if it were possible to surmount these hurdles, it seems unrealistic to believe that black youngsters can or should be persuaded to look upon caddying as a viable career choice. The African American caddie, how-

ever, has had an integral role in the development of golf in the
United States and his probably inevitable demise should be regarded
with regret. His departure will close an important chapter in sports
history.

4 | A Struggle for Self-Reliance

Barely noticeable at first, golf's popularity among the noncaddying ranks of African Americans began to emerge in the years shortly before the entry of the United States into World War I. The spread of public golf courses in cities of the Northeast provided black novices with a place to play, and gradually they began to be seen on these municipal links. Their numbers were further augmented by former caddies who had found other types of employment.

The appearance of this wave of black golfers was greeted by white players with attitudes ranging from indifference to hostility to ridicule. Perhaps the most glaring example of the latter was found in viciously racist cartoons which portrayed black golfers as buffoons and simpletons with little understanding of the game. Not only were these images depicted in adult publications, but they also appeared in children's literature of the period.(1) Nevertheless, the shameful behavior of racial bigots could not dampen the ardor of African Americans for the game nor prevent them from playing golf whenever the opportunity presented itself.

As the nation entered into the second decade of the twentieth century, changes were taking place in the country's demographics that would produce an upsurge in the number of black golfers. "Within the brief period of three years following the outbreak of the great war in Europe, more than four hundred thousand negroes suddenly moved north." These words, written by the eminent black scholar-writer Emmett J. Scott, reveal that the movement " . . .

An illustration of black golfers for a children's book published in 1897. Such demeaning stereotypes of African Americans were commonplace in printed material during that period.

swept on thousands of the blacks from the remote regions of the South, depopulated entire communities, drew upon the negro inhabitants of practically every city of the South and spread from Florida to the western limits of Texas."(2) The African American newspaper *Chicago Defender* actively encouraged the Southern exodus, and its weekly editions during these years were eagerly awaited and read with great interest by large numbers of dissatisfied blacks longing for relief from their misery. This huge migration would have a significant impact on black participation in the game of golf.

Although the number of available golf courses was relatively small, the opportunities to play (which formerly were nonexistent for blacks who did not caddie) now became a distinct possibility for that group of new migrants. Moreover, within the swollen ranks of African Americans living in northeastern and midwestern cities were a goodly number who had caddied in the South before they left. Though now working at other jobs, their love of the game went undiminished. In fact, it is reasonable to assume that they were more anxious than ever to play in surroundings where they faced fewer restrictions than when they caddied below the Mason-Dixon line. For both those who had caddied previously and those who had not, the major issue was finding enough money to buy equipment and pay green fees. Access was no longer the paramount concern.

As their numbers grew, it was only a matter of time before black golfers in various localities began to come together to form clubs. Sometime before 1910 in Chicago, Walter Speedy and others formed the Pioneer Golf Club. Within the next five years, a second black association, the Alpha Golf Club, was formed in the same city. An indication of their keen interest in the game can be gleaned from a 1915 newspaper article which reported: "The Alpha Golf Club journeyed [50 miles] to Rockford, Ill., Thursday, November 4, in their autos to see Theo. Pankey play DeFay, the upper state champion . . . "(3)

Considering the hardships of road travel in those days, the Alpha members were hearty souls indeed to endure a 100-mile round-trip automobile journey to observe a golf match. By 1921, golf's attractiveness as a sport for African Americans had grown to the extent that an article in the *Chicago Defender* stated: " . . . the reason for its popularity is that golf captivates from the instant one begins to play."

John M. Shippen (fourth from the left) with members of the Royal Golf Club of Washington D.C. Circa 1930.
(Credit: Dr. and Mrs. Walter Combs)

Becoming even more effusive, the writer concluded the brief article with an outburst of flowery prose, declaring: " . . . In short, it is the universal game—the superlative in athletics—the most democratic, the most rational, the most exhilarating, beneficial and enjoyable pastime yet invented by man." Few sports could claim such extravagant praise.

Under the leadership of a small number of farsighted male and female black golfers, new associations began to proliferate, particularly on the East Coast. In 1926, Dr. J. R. Anderson was instrumental in organizing New York City's St. Nicholas Golf Club. The following year, Philadelphia businessman Augustus Tanksley was joined by five others to form Fairview Golf Club. Not to be left behind, in Washington, D.C., dentist Albert Harris, physician George Adams, Harry Jackson, and Beltran Parker were the driving forces behind the 1928 formation of the Capital City Golf Club. In 1930, Charles Thoroughgood and his wife, Laura, harnessed the support of a few playing companions to form the New Amsterdam Golf Club, the second prominent golf group in New York City. That same year, the Capital City Golf Club disbanded and many of its former members merged with a second group of golfers to establish the Royal Golf Club. These four East Coast golf clubs became an important power bloc in black golf circles, and their combined influence would be felt for years to come.

Information is sparse concerning the early development of black golf clubs in the Midwest outside of the Chicago area. One newspaper article indicated that a group of black golfers in the upper Midwest came together sometime in the late 1920s or very early 1930s to form the Central States Golf Association. Apparently based in Minneapolis, Minnesota, this group was also comprised of members living in Iowa, Kansas, Missouri, and Nebraska. A September 1932 issue of another African American newspaper carried a report of an Omaha, Nebraska golf group being victorious in a match with the Valley Club of Des Moines, Iowa.(4) From the little that is known about black golfing activities in the Southwest and Far West in the years immediately following World War I, it is improbable that organizational structures were in place before the late 1930s.

For the most part, black golf clubs, although constituted with formally adopted rules of governance, were more akin to social gatherings of like-minded individuals who met at regular intervals to promote a common interest. Few of the organizations owned the places where they met and, as a result, they were compelled to conduct their affairs wherever they could get together in relative privacy. This usually meant using the meeting rooms of churches, libraries, or civic and community organizations. Not infrequently, they held meetings in rotation at the homes of members. As time passed, a few organizations such as the Fairview and Royal Golf Clubs bought buildings where meetings could be held and organizational records maintained. The majority, however, were unable or unwilling to do so. This failure to secure a dedicated physical facility would later prove to be a deterrent to the establishment of organizational memory, and it contributed to the instability of many black golf groups.

On October 7, 1915, what was described as the "first Negro National Golf Tournament" was played on the Marquette Park Golf Course in Chicago. It was sponsored by the Alpha Golf Club, and it was won by Walter Speedy.(5) Newspaper accounts did not indicate how many players participated on that cold blustery day, but one paper did say that players from coast to coast took part. However, it seems unlikely that it stirred a great deal of interest because 10 years would pass before another such event would be staged.

Within a few months after the Marquette Park tournament was held, the first of two significant developments in the sporting world occurred that would affect African American golfers. On January 16, 1916, at a meeting sponsored by millionaire merchant Rodman Wanamaker, the Professional Golfers' Association of America (PGA) was formed. The PGA and the United States Golf Association (USGA), which had been established in 1894, became the governing authorities for amateur and professional golf in the United States. Neither showed much interest in the activities or concerns of black golfers who continued to languish outside the orbit of a recognized governing structure.

In late 1916, the black tennis world began to take decisive action to develop a national tennis organization. Even though the United States Lawn Tennis Association had come into existence in 1881, it paid little or no attention to issues and problems confronting African American tennis players—just like its counterparts in golf. In contrast to their golf counterparts, however, black tennis players took steps to improve the situation. Toward the latter part of the year, at a banquet held in Harlem, New York, the idea of a national tennis organization was proposed. A temporary planning group was formed and on November 1, "a letter was sent to all Negro Tennis Clubs known to be functioning in the United States, inviting them to send representatives to a meeting to be held in Washington, D. C. on November 30, 1916 at 10 o'clock A. M." Out of that meeting, the American Tennis Association (ATA) came into being.(6)

In the same way that black golfers were not quick to follow the example set by their tennis-playing colleagues in establishing a national organization, they were very slow in staging another national golf tournament after the 1915 event. It was not until Labor Day weekend of 1925 that the next major golf tournament took place. At the Shady Rest Golf and Country Club in Westfield, New Jersey, Harry Jackson led a field of golfers from Connecticut, the District of Columbia, New York, and Pennsylvania to win the two-day competition. The event was successful enough, however, that it was decided to do it again the following year at another location. The site chosen was the Mapledale Country Club in Stow, Massachusetts, owned by Robert Hawkins.

There are slightly differing versions about the origin of the first (and only) national black golf organization. But as best as can be reconstructed, the organization's chronology began in early to mid-1925. At that time, a group of black golfers meeting in Washington, D.C. formed the United States Colored Golf Association (USCGA). There is no evidence that Hawkins was a member of that group. After the Labor Day tournament that year, B. C. Gordon, who was president of the Shady Rest Golf & Country Club, was elected president of the USCGA.

When the event was scheduled for Mapledale, it appears that both Hawkins and the USCGA became actively involved in recruiting players. It is unclear, however, who was in charge, or if distinct lines of authority were ever established. From all indications there were few problems, so the tournament returned to Mapledale in 1927 and 1928. Sometime during this period the words "States" and "Colored" were deleted from the organization's title. At the conclusion of the 1928 tournament, Dr. George Adams of Washington, D. C. was elected temporary president. In 1929, the Labor Day tourna-

Dr. George Adams, a founding member of the UGA
and ardent supporter of the Wake-Robin Golf Club.
(Credit: Dr. Elizabeth Brabble)

ment returned to Shady Rest and, after it ended, the United Golfers Association (UGA) became a permanent organization, with Dr. Ernest J. Ricks of Chicago installed as its first president. Hawkins never became president of the organization, but there is little doubt that he worked selflessly and energetically to establish a national black golf organization.

In order to circumvent the apartheid-like structure of organized sports that existed for much of the first half of the twentieth century, African Americans were compelled to rely on their own (albeit limited) resources. Public golf courses, though increasing in number, were insufficient to meet the demands of a growing golfing community. Rich white golfers could build private courses to satisfy their needs, but those less wealthy often encountered difficulties gaining access to suitable facilities.

For black golfers, the situation was particularly irritating and it led to repeated attempts to secure ownership of country clubs and golf courses. These undertakings are the subject of an excellent study by sociology professor Marvin P. Dawkins. Relying heavily on articles printed in African American newspapers at the height of the segregation era, Dawkins explains why enforced segregation fostered the formation of a separate and distinct African American world of golf. Drawing on concepts espoused by fellow scholar J. E. Blackwell, Dawkins argues that when black golfers were excluded from the white organizations their only alternative was to develop separate organizations. Referred to as "parallel structures," the entities that were formed to serve the needs of black constituents could not avoid resembling those in the mainstream golf community.(7) The UGA was an example *par excellence* of a "parallel structure." Another was the African American-owned country club or golf course.

The country club is a distinctly American social institution. Eagerly yearning to emulate the style and elegance of British aristocracy, rich Americans of the late 1800s sought ways to display the wealth they had acquired in the age of industrialization. Unfortunately, the *nouveau riche* of the United States did not possess that important symbol of British aristocratic tradition—the country house set on a vast rural estate. Nevertheless, as American cities expanded, affluent residents began to acquire land in the suburbs that was large enough to accommodate a wide range of outdoor sports.

Gradually a pattern began to emerge. "In the 1880s clubs sprang up on the outskirts of major cities drawing their original membership from each city's wealthy, largely WASP [white, Anglo-Saxon, Protestant] elite."(8) Golf became an important activity in those clubs and within 15 years nearly 40 country clubs had golf courses. It was not long before golf became a defining feature of country club culture. Established by the WASP elite, the country club was a bastion of exclusivity. Even today, when a number of white country clubs have relaxed religious and gender restrictions, very few African Americans have gained membership. In the 1920s, the barriers were virtually insurmountable. During those years, only by "passing" for white could someone of African descent join a country club. It was in this stifling

racial atmosphere that sports-minded African Americans were compelled to develop alternatives.

The first documented country club owned by African Americans
was the Shady Rest Golf & Country Club in New Jersey. Organized
on September 21, 1921, the history of Shady Rest dates back to
1900 with the opening of the white-owned Westfield Country Club
and its nine-hole golf course. Located in the town of Scotch Plains
some 12 miles southwest of Newark, New Jersey, the club encom-
passed 31 acres on Jerusalem Road at the northern end of the Westfield railroad line.

As time passed, a number of black families established a small
community surrounding the club and frequently they would walk
across sections of the golf course to visit friends and relatives living
nearby. In doing so, the community residents established a type of
easement known as a "right to travel." When the nine-hole layout
had outgrown the golfing needs of the Westfield membership, plans
were considered for expanding it into an 18-hole course. To do so,
however, would require the erection of barriers that would interfere
with the "right to travel." Unwilling to become embroiled in a legal
battle with the surrounding black community, and after many
months of debate, the Westfield owners decided to locate elsewhere
and to sell the property to the Progressive Realty Corporation, a
group of prominent African American investors. The Westfield
Country Club became the Shady Rest Golf & Country Club.

Some club members and other white residents of Westfield were
angry about the decision and were willing to share their views with
anyone who cared to listen. Rumors of their dissatisfaction with having to tolerate a black social resort in their midst began to circulate
and eventually came to the attention of the New York City press.
Nine months after the sale, a reporter from the *New York Sun* visited
Shady Rest and the town of Westfield to see if he could learn " . . . .
what strange combination of circumstances brought this social cata-
clysm to pass in the heart of aristocratic Union County?"

One of the people the reporter interviewed was E. S. F. Randolph,
a white real estate dealer who was reputed to be the largest property
owner in the town. With his impudent pen and irreverent style, the
reporter noted " . . . Mr. Randolph didn't seem perturbed over the
menace of a negro social colony." Even more revealing were Ran-

dolph's comments that the new owners " . . . agreed to pay us a good price—more than we had originally paid for it . . . They're meeting their payments," Randolph concluded, "and we're satisfied."(9)

In addition to its importance as the first of its kind, Shady Rest Golf & Country Club had amenities that set it apart from other clubs. Besides golf, it offered six tennis courts, croquet, horseback riding, and skeet shooting. Indoors it contained a large dining room, locker room facilities, a reception hall, a ballroom, and several meeting rooms. Viewed as a social phenomenon, Shady Rest had some interesting internal contradictions. Owned and operated by an emerging black middle class, its club policies were a curious combination of elitism and populism. While it became a meeting place for the African American social set of the East Coast, Shady Rest was not unmindful of its responsibility to respond to the social and recreational needs of the local African American community. This unusual degree of social consciousness prompted one observer in the June 23, 1923, issue of the *Pittsburgh Courier* to remark that "The fact that Saturdays are given to visitors at a 75 cents admission is in itself an indication that the club is inclined to democratic policies . . . "

New York University history professor Dr. Jeffrey Sammons supports this observation and thinks that Shady Rest fulfilled a community function that comparable white country clubs were unwilling to assume. Additionally, Professor Sammons contends that in contrast to Shady Rest, white country clubs were (and still are) more isolated from their local communities. Consequently, local citizens neither look upon the nearby country club as a community institution nor share any interest or pride in what takes place there.(10)

Despite a rocky period in the 1920s when a bitter dispute arose over control of the club, followed by the devastating effects of the Great Depression, Shady Rest managed to survive until 1963. No longer able to function as an African American social institution, Shady Rest became a public facility and its name was changed to the Scotch Hills Country Club. During its life of more than 40 years, Shady Rest was more than what is commonly associated with the country club ambiance. It provided an unusually wide range of recreational activities; it served as an important intellectual oasis; it provided memorable musical entertainment; it was the venue for nu-

merous black golf tournaments; and it was the final place of employment for the legendary black golf professional, John Shippen.

The full significance of Shady Rest Golf & Country Club is diminished, however, if it is taken out of historical context. Seldom remembered or mentioned, Shady Rest's acquisition by black Americans in 1921 occurred slightly more than three months after a
barbaric riot in Tulsa, Oklahoma. On one terrible June night,
10,000 crazed, armed whites went on an orgy of killing, burning,
and pillaging that left more than 100 blacks dead (an accurate death
toll has never been determined), untold numbers injured, and 35
blocks of Tulsa's black community destroyed.(11) Though more
than 1,000 miles away from the Oklahoma holocaust, the new owners of Shady Rest and the black residents in the surrounding community were not untouched by the hideous events that had transpired in
the boomtown of oil barons. Yet, with perseverance and indomitable
faith in the future, they pursued the goal of self-reliance. Shady Rest
is a testament to those beliefs.

Mapledale Country Club in Stow, Massachusetts is another
African American-owned country club worthy of attention. Opened
in 1926 some 25 miles from Boston, the property was part of a
sumptuous estate once owned by a physician-friend of President
John Quincy Adams. The driving force behind the acquisition of
Mapledale was Robert H. Hawkins, president of the board of direc-
tors. A stockily built man with a round face and an engaging personality, Hawkins had worked for many years at white country clubs in
the Boston area. He was optimistic that the new venture would be
successful because he had obtained the support of " . . . .a group of
colored people who are forging ahead in material things."(12) Initially there was reason for optimism. In the first week of September
of 1928, Mapledale hosted the third open golf championship of the
USCGA. A total of $300 in prize money was awarded, and the top
professional received $100. At the conclusion of the event there was
an elaborate program/dinner dance, and prizes awarded for the
longest drive, best dressed golfer, and for the owner of the "best
looking set of clubs."

By 1929, however, Hawkins was a disillusioned man. He had
spent $25,000 of his personal funds and had borrowed an additional
$5,000 to keep the club alive. As the months passed, he became in-

creasingly embittered by what was described as a "failure on the part of Negroes in Boston and the immediate vicinity to support Mapledale . . . " In the spring of that year, Hawkins wrote a lengthy explanation about why he had decided to abandon the venture. In it, he expressed disappointment with individuals whom he felt had circulated misinformation about his management of club affairs. Perhaps he was saddened most by a newspaper account of his decision, which read in part, " Mapledale Country Club at Stow will no longer be a resort for colored people. On March 31 and in the future it will be known as the Stow Golf and Country Club, Inc.; henceforth it will cater to white people only . . . "(13)

A year before Hawkins decided to abandon the Stow enterprise, three wealthy African American businessmen in Los Angeles, California combined their assets to purchase the Parkridge Country Club in the southern part of the state. The club grounds comprised 289 acres of prime property, and the total estate was in excess of 650 acres. The clubhouse was described as, "a magnificent structure of stucco and steel construction, standing atop the hill, a majestic sight to be seen from far distant points. It is a monument to the stability and financial integrity of the progressive Negro." The club contained an 18-hole golf course and a separate 9-hole layout for use by beginners. The grounds also contained a large swimming pool and several tennis courts. On some of the land, "fifty small bungalows, completely furnished" had been erected and plans had been discussed for subdividing a portion of the remaining property for larger home construction. Apparently the owners were also interested in using part of the land (dotted with orange groves) for agricultural purposes since mention was made of the availability of sufficient water for irrigation.(14) Unfortunately, the subsequent history of the Parkridge venture is not known. It is likely that plans for the future failed to materialize and with its demise went the dreams of another group of African Americans intent on pursuing the goal of institutional self-reliance.

Although most of the attempts by African Americans to secure permanent ownership of golf courses eventually foundered, there were a few success stories. When he returned home to Stark County, Ohio shortly after the end of World War II, William Powell formed a partnership with two black physicians to buy a small fruit farm on

Route 30 near the town of East Canton. His goal was to build a golf course in the town that had barred him from playing many years earlier.

A versatile athlete in his youth, Powell had caddied while in elementary school and later captained his high school golf and football teams. He spent a short time in college but was unable to finish due to lack of funds. Powell obtained janitorial employment at the local Timken roller bearing factory, but within a few months he was promoted to become the first black security guard on the company police force. Not long after the United States entered the war, he was drafted for military service and was sent to England.

When he returned from his tour of overseas duty, Powell went back to his old job at Timken. He also spent months trying to obtain a veteran's loan. All of the banks in Canton denied his requests, and his hopes all but vanished until the two doctors came to his rescue. After two years of backbreaking toil at night and on weekends—working at Timken during the week—William Powell opened the nine-hole Clearview Golf Course in the spring of 1948. He and his wife, Marcella, built a modest house on the course and raised a daughter, Renee, and a son, Lawrence. Saving as much as possible from his salaried job at the factory and living frugally, Powell bought out his physician partners in the late 1960s. In the 1970s (he cannot remember the exact year), he expanded the course to its present size of 18 holes measuring nearly 6,100 yards in length.(15)

A retiring but outspoken man, Powell is equally proud of the golfing achievements of his daughter, whom he began teaching at the age of three. In 1967, Renee Powell joined the Ladies Professional Golf Association Tour (LPGA) and remained an active competitor for 13 years. After a stint as a golf professional in England, Renee returned to become the professional at Clearview, since her father was no longer able to continue in that role. It was gratifying to her family that she chose to follow the courageous and visionary path of William Powell. Because of him, Clearview Golf Course is one of the four known remaining golf courses in the United States that are owned and operated by African Americans.

The Greater Philadelphia Golf and Country Club was established to acquire, own, manage, and develop leisure and recreational facilities and was incorporated in 1967. The corporation's founding

A composite picture of Renee Powell relaxing and in action, circa 1977.
(Credit: AP/World Wide Photo)

members were Maxwell Stanford, Robert Salisbury, Albert Letson, and J. Lester Blocker. Shortly after its formation, the corporation bought the 136-acre Turnersville Golf Course in Sicklerville, New Jersey. After its purchase, the name of the 18-hole championship course located 15 miles outside Philadelphia was changed to the Freeway Golf Course. Play on the course began in August of 1968, and the following year it was the site of the 43rd Annual Championship of the UGA. Over the years, a number of major corporations have used Freeway for company-sponsored tournaments. Entering its thirtieth consecutive year in existence, this African American-owned golf course has withstood numerous financial challenges. Its mere survival is a notable achievement and, with a bit of good fortune, Freeway Golf Course should reach its full potential.

A third black-owned golf course is a newcomer to the scene. The Bull Creek Golf and Country Club in Louisburg, North Carolina opened for play on October 10, 1996. Located on 170 acres, the land is owned jointly by five families—the Massenburgs, Solomons,

Keiths, Stricklands, and Browns—and in earlier years it was used for raising tobacco and hogs. In 1992, family members pooled their resources, hired consultants, and agreed that construction of a golf course would be a prudent investment. After months of delays, the first nine holes and the driving range were finally completed.(16) Short-range plans call for completing the remaining nine holes within two years. Long- range plans call for the construction of a pro shop, swimming pool, and tennis and basketball courts.

The nine-hole Meadowbrook Country Club in Garner, North Carolina, is the only other black-owned golf course known to be in existence.

At one time or another, nearly 30 golf courses were owned by African Americans. Not included in this list are the Crescent City Country Club in New Orleans, Louisiana, the Bayou Bend Boat and Country Club in Houston, Texas, and the Haywood Country Club in Brownsville, Tennessee. Although there were press reports that these properties had been purchased by African Americans, there is no evidence that the courses ever opened for play. There may have been an additional half dozen or more courses, but they have proved difficult to trace. Other than the few that exist today, virtually all were built or purchased before 1950. The overwhelming majority were located in the eastern half of the United States, and more than one-quarter had at least 18 holes.

Why did so many of them fail? There is reason to believe that all but a very few were undercapitalized at the onset, and their financial projections were overly optimistic. It is not known to what extent the owners had conducted preliminary market surveys, but almost without exception the new golf courses were unable to attract vitally needed investors or members. Although many of the owners had been involved with other businesses, few had the experience to manage an enterprise of such complexity. While there is no clear evidence of deliberate tampering with financial records, unacceptable accounting practices could have led to some failures.

How much of an impact racial prejudice had on the eventual outcomes is difficult to ascertain. It was (and is) an ever-present feature of American life, and unquestionably it was a factor if owners had to deal with adversarial white lawyers or enter into financial negotiations with reluctant white lending institutions. Yet . . . credit worthiness, marginal resources, and managerial competence are issues that cannot be dismissed. Inevitably, the question is: Would any of the failed ventures have survived if the owners had been white? Maybe, maybe not.

5 | Between the Wars

One of the early references to golf in an African American newspaper appeared in a 1911 issue of the *New York Age*. Although the article was published outside the chronological boundaries set for this chapter, it is being discussed at this point because it illustrates one of the many problems faced by black golfers before (and after) 1917.

In the strictest sense, the article was actually an *advertisement* prepared for publication by E. W. Dale, owner and proprietor of the Hotel Dale in Cape May, New Jersey. In a promotional style not uncommon during the era, businessman Dale proudly stated that his establishment was ". . . the finest and most complete hostelry in the United States for the accommodation of our race . . ." He stated further that Hotel Dale ". . . was located on an elevated site . . . opposite the widely celebrated Cape May Golf Club . . ." Dale's advertisement also mentioned that the front of the hotel overlooked the golf links. In addition to "sea bathing," prospective vacationers could play tennis or croquet, and arrangements could be made for them to fish or sail.(1) Left unsaid, however, was any mention of guests having *access* to the (white-owned) links that were so "widely celebrated." In truth, if black golfers wanted to enjoy the ambiance of Hotel Dale, they would either have to find an alternative to the golf course there at the hotel's doorstep, or leave their equipment at home.

Black golfers, however, had no intention of being banished from the game they loved so dearly. In 1915, E. L. Renip, the enthusiastic golf editor of the *Chicago Defender,* wrote about an outstanding round of golf played by one of the Windy City's better black golfers at a course in outlying Evanston. "Laurie Ayton," Renip wrote, " did a little golfing out at the Evanston course the other day that probably will stand as a record for all time at that sporty course." Renip obviously believed that Ayton's score of two-under-par deserved to be widely publicized. Not known for his reticence or the use of measured language, Renip felt obliged to share his excitement with the readership. Renip's comments indicate that golf was not an unknown sport in the black community. Even though their numbers were relatively small, black Americans interested in the game played with the "crooked stick" could not be ignored. In fact, the contagion of the sport was becoming visible in other cities. In 1921, a sportswriter for the *Chicago Defender* who was covering athletic events in New York City reported: "George Aaron and Arthur Gibbs of the New York Colored Golf Club have finished a successful season at the Van Cortlandt links . . . "(2)

Evidence of the growing interest in golf by blacks continued to mount to the extent that another national open tournament was planned for September of 1922. When the tournament was first announced, special efforts were made to be certain that anyone could participate regardless of race, creed, or color. Having suffered the humiliation of racial prejudice at local, regional, and national events, the Windy City Golf Association (the tournament hosts) declared forthrightly that it would not tolerate racial exclusion in any event with which it was associated. Although few whites were inclined to enter black-run golf tournaments, the nondiscrimination principle became firmly established, and it would be enunciated repeatedly without equivocation in the future.

As the 1920s rolled on, articles about golf began to appear with increasing frequency in African American newspapers. Golf events in the Midwest and on the East Coast were reported during most of the summer months, and the game began to be included in the range of sporting activities for blacks to play and enjoy. "Spring is here," wrote respected columnist Floyd J. Calvin in the May 3, 1924 issue of the *Pittsburgh Courier,* [and] "The soft and invigorating zephyrs that we longed for in mid-winter have come at last . . . golf, baseball, fishing, tennis . . . and many other forms of recreation and merry making are in season once more."

Throughout the twentieth century many voices were raised to protest racial prejudice in golf. One of the early black critics was William de Hart Hubbard. A former track star at the University of Michigan, Hubbard won the 1924 Olympic gold medal for the long jump in Paris, France, and for many years he was an outstanding competitor in other track and field events. In 1925 and 1926, Hubbard wrote a series of sports articles for the *Pittsburgh Courier*. His first article dealt with racial prejudice in sports. After tackling the problem as it occurred in boxing, Hubbard shifted to golf. His comments were profound and quite accurate. The heading asked: "What Will Golf Do?"

To turn to another field, the colored man has not, as yet, presented a problem in the golf world. The reason is not hard to find. Golf, until recently, has been a rich man's game. The enormous amount of ground needed for a playing course, the expense of upkeep and other incidental expenses kept the man of lesser wealth out of the game of hit the ball and look for it. Very, very few of our race could afford the expense of the game and those who could were not likely to be admitted to the expensive white clubs. So the Negro stayed out of golf.

But now things have changed. The ancient game of Scottish kings has become too popular to remain exclusive. Many of the large cities of the North have built public courses and so have opened the game for the poorer man. Our people have responded. Go to Chicago, Detroit, Cleveland or any city with a public course and you will see colored players enjoying the game. They are not yet as proficient as their white brethren, but they are progressing rapidly. The colored man is taking up golf and he is bound to develop some star players.

That reminds me of an article I saw in the papers last spring. I forgot whether it was Detroit or Cleveland that had their Public Links Caddy Tournament. Anyway, there were a number of colored caddies on the course and they saw no reason why they should not take part in the tourney. They entered and the surprises began. Instead of being eliminated at the start as the

whites expected, they started off winning matches. Once in a
while a colored player was eliminated but only after a hard
fight. The outcome was that a white caddy (sic) and a colored
caddy (sic) were finalists. The white boy won but the match
went to extra holes.

I have heard many comments on the golfing proficiency of
some of the colored caddies on the Southern courses. Long association with the game is bound to bring proficiency. Then,
too, there are few private colored country clubs where they (il-
legible) may take up the game. It will not be long before   we
have some top notch players. Will they get their chances in the
big championship tournaments of the country? Maybe, but not
likely. We will probably have to have colored golf tournaments
just as we now have colored tennis championships, and baseball
championships.(3)

Remarkably prescient, Hubbard was not sanguine about prospects
for eradicating the blight of racial prejudice from golf. Yet, he was
not totally despondent. He felt certain that if given the opportunity,
black golfers, especially the younger ones, would rise to the challenge and eventually excel. On the other hand, he was realistic
enough to appreciate that, for the foreseeable future, black golfers
would have to rely on their own institutions and resources as they
strived for justice and parity.

There is little doubt that the tournament held in Stow, Massachusetts, in 1926 kindled considerable interest in the black golf community. By July of the following year the Bunker Club was organized in
Pittsburgh and it led one newspaper to headline: "Golf To Become
Major Sport Here." The accompanying article contained an odd
statement open to various interpretations. While acknowledging that
the Schenley Park Golf Course in Pittsburgh was a public facility, the
article reports that ". . . steps have been made to secure the use of
these links at a special time to *not* (writer's emphasis) avoid any conflict with other groups." Were the black golfers who intended to play
on the Schenley Park course hoping to provoke a confrontation? Or
was the word "*not*" inserted by accident? Given the prevailing racial
atmosphere in 1927, it probably was an error. Yet one cannot over-
look the unlikely possibility that one or more of the group's militant

members were willing to challenge the denial of access to a public facility. Subsequent issues of the newspaper did not carry a correction or disclaimer. Neither was there a report of any disruption, protest, or incident.

Another item of interest appeared as a photograph in a June 1927 issue of the *Chicago Defender*. It showed a youngish black man holding a golf club. The caption beneath the photograph read:

Dorsey Adams. Twenty-five year old golf expert from Daytona, Fla., who was employed as an assistant pro at the exclusive Claredon Golf Club, rising from caddie to caddiemaster, to assistant professional. Tex Rickard sent for Adams and he is now teaching the big town folks on the top of Madison Square Garden, New York City.(4)

Boxing promoter and sportsman Rickard was a notable personality in sporting circles during this period, and he was well acquainted with the golf world. He recognized talent when he saw it and obviously believed that the young Floridian would be a successful golf instructor in New York. Nothing further, unfortunately, was heard of Adams, suggesting that life in the big city did not fulfill his expectations.

One of the striking aspects of African American golf history is the significant expansion of player participation that occurred after the stock market crash of 1929. Conspicuously absent, unfortunately, is any mention—much less discussion—of this phenomenon in the sports literature of the period. Consequently, the answer to the question of how black golfers—who were part of society's most vulnerable segment—were able to increase their numbers in the midst of the Great Depression is a puzzle even today. But that's exactly what happened.

The tempo of activities quickened commensurate with the continuing increase in the number of black golfers and black golf groups. In 1930, it was reported that the 72-hole Eastern Open Tournament would take place at Shady Rest Golf & Country Club on July 4th and 5th. Plans were also announced for a match to be played on July 6th between the leading eastern golfers and competitors from Bermuda. As far as it is known, this was the first formal golf event involving African Americans and players from another country. Other tournaments took place in Philadelphia and New York. The season ended with the UGA national tournament at the Casa Loma Country Club in Power's Lake, Wisconsin on August 30th and 31st. A cryptic paragraph in a June issue of the *Chicago Defender* stated: "It is likely that an eastern golf association will be organized to rule the eastern open and the eastern inter-club matches."(5) The matter of a governing body was destined to come to the fore again in later years.

The 1930s also witnessed a short-lived but energetic campaign to develop miniature golf. Sparked by the *Pittsburgh Courier* newspaper, the new fad was promoted as an indoor sport that could be played year round without requiring a substantial financial outlay for equipment, green fees, and travel. The thrust of miniature golf advertisements strongly suggested that the new sport was intended to rival conventional golf. Fortunately for the traditional game, miniature golf did not attract many followers outside of Pittsburgh—and even there its popularity plummeted within 18 months. The brief episode clearly illustrated that the standard game of golf had a loyal and steady following in the African American community. Miniature golf was never a serious rival for its affection.

In 1932, a somewhat unusual development occurred that is not clearly understood. Undercurrents of discord within the UGA began to surface soon after the organization was founded in 1925. Unfortunately, it is difficult to pinpoint specific areas of disagreement. Nevertheless, by February of 1932 the situation had reached the stage where some type of action was considered necessary. Under the leadership of Charles Thoroughgood, representatives from the Fairview, New Amsterdam, Royal, and St. Nicholas golf clubs met in Philadelphia to form the Eastern Golf Association (EGA). They elected Leonard Kennerly as its first president. Even though it remained affiliated with the UGA, the new organization made it clear that it intended to exert its semi-autonomous authority over black golfing activities in the East. Unambiguously, the EGA declared that its " . . . supervision of golf extends as far south as Virginia and as far north as the New England States."(6) Displaying a remarkable willingness to work together, however, the major contending factions established a *modus vivendi* (compromise) that would ensure survival of both organizations. The new arrangement went a long way toward alleviating, though never completely eliminating, underlying differences. With the passage of time, additional clubs joined the EGA (and the UGA ostensibly), and this dual structure remained in existence for many years.

In 1936, *The United Golfer* magazine made its debut with the publication of its May issue. Described by its editor, John M. Lee, as a "pioneering effort," the magazine was published by the Fairview Golf Club and sold initially for 25 cents a copy. In the first issue, Augustus Tanksley, the managing editor, wrote a column proposing a complicated and thoroughly unworkable procedure for financing the publication. He proposed that the publication costs would be shared jointly by the UGA and the club responsible for hosting the annual UGA tournament. In what could be construed as a somewhat defiant gesture to the UGA's executive body, Tanksley wrote: "In case the sponsoring club or the UGA does not wish to comply with this agreement [,] then the Fairview Golf Club staff shall continue the publication of the *United Golfer Magazine*." The reactions to Tanksley's proposal are not known, but one suspects that it provoked a lively discussion in some quarters.

The black golfing public was thirsty for the material in *The United Golfer*. White golf publications seldom included items of interest for black players, so the new magazine filled a void that not even African American newspapers could provide. Noteworthy, for example, was a hole-by-hole summary of the final round of the 1936 national open championship held that year at Cobbs Creek Golf Course in Philadelphia. The contest, featuring the play of John Dendy, Zeke Hartsfield, and Howard Wheeler, was graphically reported and made enjoyable reading. Accompanying the summary was a fine photograph of John Dendy putting on the 13th green before an attentive gallery.

Subsequent issues provided a number of other good photographs, and the magazine added columns on instruction, letters to the editor, and an assortment of items concerning activities at various UGA-affiliated clubs. In 1937 an editorial reported that the magazine had been accepted as the official organ of both the UGA and EGA. Issues of the magazine continued to appear more or less regularly, with the same editorial staff, until 1938 when Joseph H. Hudson became both editor and managing editor.

John Dendy, Zeke Hartsfield and Howard Wheeler putting on the 3rd green in the final round of the 1936 UGA National Championship.

At or about the same time, in an important change of policy and format, the magazine began to include additional sports, and its name was changed to *The United Golfer and Other Sports*. With this change the magazine lost its focus, its special appeal to golfers, and its potential for becoming a recognized forum of expression for the African American golf community. Lacking sufficient editorial depth and expertise, the quality of writing—never particularly strong—deteriorated further in the attempt to cover a wider range of sports. Shortly after the end of World War II, the magazine basically ceased to exist. Perhaps it was not fully realized at the time, but the demise of *The United Golfer* would later prove to be detrimental to the interests of black golf.

If there were any lingering doubts that golf was becoming a permanent sports fixture in the African American community, they should have been dispelled by even a cursory review of developments during the 1930s. The first four annual UGA tournaments were held between 1926 and 1929, with three taking place in Massachusetts. Further proof of the sport's growing popularity was provided in a September 12, 1938, issue of *Time* magazine, which reported that there were 50,000 black golfers in the country. Another positive sign was the fact that the 1939 UGA national tournament was held in

Los Angeles, California, marking the first time the event was held on the West Coast. Some 200 entrants were registered to play and, in the style of the world's film capital, the event was captured in a motion picture documentary.(7) Befitting the Hollywood image, film celebrities such as Louise Beavers, Johnny Weismuller, Alan Mowbray, Preston Foster, Frank Capra, and Al Jolson donated trophies, and actress Hattie McDaniels presented the awards.

As the 1930s drew to a close, not only were more black golf groups being formed, but more tournaments were being held. In addition to the large annual UGA Labor Day event, smaller but no less enthusiastic tournaments were held in Philadelphia, Washington D.C., New York, Chicago, and Boston. A network of black golfers began to emerge, and residents of Louisiana, Florida, North Carolina, and Georgia were making new friends and rivals from Pennsylvania, Illinois, Connecticut, and New Jersey. The new tournament network was adding a fresh dimension to black golf that would grow and mature in the decades to follow.

There was, to be sure, another side of the coin; one that revealed flaws in the UGA, especially the way it handled the national tournaments. After the 1938 event, which was held at the Palos Park Golf Course some 20 miles from downtown Chicago, F. A. "Fay" Young, the esteemed sportswriter of the *Chicago Defender*, wrote a scathing criticism of the UGA's ineptitude and its *laissez faire* style of tournament management. He complained about many things: the failure to transmit scores to him in a timely manner; the incomplete and inaccurate score sheets; the unavailability of members of the publicity committee because they were competing in the tournament; and the general unresponsiveness to his requests for assistance. He also mentioned that " . . . there is dissension both in the Chicago club and the national organization." More ominously, he indicated that " . . . the southern players are threatening to withdraw from the U.G.A. following the attitude displayed by some Chicagoans who seek to run both the Chicago club and the U.G.A. . . . " Concluding the article, Young observed: " . . . the U.G.A. has a long way to go before it can be compared to the American Tennis Association . . . "(8) Young's criticism suggests that he was among those who believed that golf's success in attracting new black players was in spite of, rather than because of, the UGA.

To add to the turmoil of these years, the UGA was also bedeviled by dissatisfaction expressed by some amateur players. Shortly before the 1939 Los Angeles tournament, the Forest City Golf Association of Cleveland, Ohio, sponsored the Fifth Annual Ohio Amateur Golf Tournament. Dr. L. S. Evans, tournament committee chairman, announced that during the course of the three-day event a National Amateur Golf Association (NAGA) would be formed. Nothing further was heard about the new organization until the following June when a rather curious photograph appeared in the *Chicago Defender*. The picture showed M. B. Bivens, who had been elected president of the NAGA, standing next to Ralph Chilton, president of the UGA. The caption beneath the photograph indicated that Bivens was relinquishing his position to support the UGA.(9) Undoubtedly, a great deal of fence-mending (and possibly arm-twisting) had taken place over the intervening months to enable a reconciliation to take place.

The absence of any further news about the NAGA suggests that it eventually disbanded, even though the so-called National Amateur Golf Tournaments continued until at least 1942 with the Forest City Golf Association actively involved. Having weathered another period of disarray, the UGA continued to stage annual tournaments until that same year, when the effects of World War II forced suspension of the events.

6 | World War II and Return to Peacetime

The Armed Forces and Black Golf

When the nation went to war after the bombing of Pearl Harbor in 1941, there was a buildup in military strength that would result in over one million black men and women being mobilized for military service before the conflict ended. With sports an important part of training and recreation, the athletic field at a military installation was often the first place that white and black personnel had contact with one another. At the onset of hostilities, few suspected that the military would become an arena of social change and would play a significant role in the history of black golf.

Somewhat surprisingly, a fairly good picture of military athletic activities can be obtained from such publications as *Army and Navy Review, Army and Navy Journal,* and from many unclassified official government documents. These publications also provide information on the athletic performance of African American soldiers as far back as the 1890s. From them, we learn that in those earlier days the most popular sports among black troops were baseball, football, basketball, boxing, and track and field. In the winter months, especially in the northern and western states, black soldiers also engaged in ice skating, gymnastics, bowling, and billiards.(1) Relatively unknown, though, is the important role the military played in the evolution of golf in society as a whole. Some of the nation's finest golfers played while serving in the armed forces, and many thousands more were introduced to the game during their years of service. Until recently, however, the golf experiences of African American servicemen and servicewomen were quite different.

In the early days, golf was slow to take hold in the military services. Where it did, the field grade officer seems to have taken the lead in promoting the sport. The decision to build a golf course at a military installation usually rested with the commanding officer. Knowing that the federal government did not permit the expenditure of appropriated funds for such projects, a commander who was a golfing enthusiast had to devise clever ways to circumvent the restrictions. He resorted to ingenious methods to secure the use of equipment and personnel without reflecting them in official reports. As golf gained popularity with his senior colleagues, an installation's commanding officer who sought to construct a course could almost be certain that he would receive sympathetic consideration from golf-loving superiors.

Before World War II, unless enlisted personnel received a special invitation, most military golf courses were restricted to use by officers *and* racially segregated. Since few black servicemen knew how to play, and fewer were interested in learning, the armed forces had no reason to promote golf among African American troops. Between the two World Wars, golf in the military was essentially a white, male sport reserved for officers and possibly their dependents.

The situation changed dramatically during World War II. After large numbers of men were drafted for military service, golf instruction became an integral part of recreational programs, and golf professionals were hired to teach new recruits (primarily white). Some of the leading professional golfers of the time, such as Byron Nelson, Harold "Jug" McSpaden, and Joe Kirkwood, played exhibition matches to help raise money for the war effort. A number of other golf fund-raising activities were staged to promote the sport in camps and at military hospitals. As a result, it was estimated that some 200,000 troops were introduced to golf during the war.(2) There was also a large group of servicemen who had played before they were drafted. Among that group were already-proficient African American golfers such as Ted Rhodes, Howard Wheeler, Bill Spiller, Charlie Sifford, and Calvin Searles, who was killed in action in

France. Still rigidly segregated, however, the military offered few opportunities for black golfers to play regularly, and it would remain that way until the end of the war. Nevertheless, using the resourcefulness that was a hallmark of their perseverance, some black servicemen were not to be denied.

—m— —m—

One example of golfing resolve during the war is shown by the exploits of retired army staff sergeant Martin "Tex" Guillory. A voluble, short-statured man with a salty tongue, Guillory was born in Galveston, Texas. Before entering the army in 1940, Guillory caddied at Galveston Country Club where he developed a reputation as one of the better ball-strikers. After the attack on Pearl Harbor, Guillory was attached to a quartermaster unit and assigned to many of the war zones in the Pacific. Rising to the rank of corporal, the wily former caddie became thoroughly familiar with ways to manipulate military rules and regulations. Thanks to the assistance of a friendly supply sergeant, Guillory found a way to take his golf clubs with him during the war. In a 1994 interview, Guillory made a remarkable admission: "I was the only soldier on Guadalcanal with golf clubs." After the island was secured from the Japanese, he also used his ingenuity to find a way to actually play the game he loved. "A few of us got together," he remembered, "and built a three-hole course so we could play a few rounds during our off time."(3)

Another example of the determination shown by black golfers in the military during World War II was demonstrated at Fort Huachuca, Arizona. Fort Huachuca was the home station of the all-black 92nd Infantry Division which later fought in Italy. In contrast to most bases, Fort Huachuca was one of the few military installations where blacks could play golf. This would have been impossible, however, without the efforts of First Lieutenant Wayne Howard of the Detachment Medical Department, who petitioned the army to build an 18-hole course at the Arizona camp. Through a combination of political savvy, persistence, and luck, he convinced his superiors that the course should be built.

—m— —m—

When President Harry Truman issued Executive Orders 9980 and 9981 on July 26, 1948, which desegregated the U.S. Armed Forces and the U. S. Civil Service, he set in motion a chain of events that would have a profound effect on race relations in the country. Even though the U. S. War Department had issued a 1943 directive forbidding the assignment of any military recreational facility on the basis of race, it was rarely enforced. Faced with mounting pressure from African American leaders, Truman's new orders were unambiguous and bore every indication that they would be implemented with vigor. Noted historian John Hope Franklin observed: "In several significant ways [the desegregation orders of] President Harry S. Truman contributed to the climate in which the status of African Americans could be improved."(4) Truman's actions were a prelude to the events that followed in the civil rights era of the 1950s and 1960s, and they changed the underlying character of the armed forces and the civil service. An important by-product of the military desegregation order was the opportunity it provided for hundreds of black personnel to become involved with the game of golf.

Almost immediately, Truman's executive orders changed the atmosphere for African Americans on military golf courses. Both black and white military personnel who were on active duty at the time say that within weeks after issuance of the orders, African Americans began to use military golf facilities in greater numbers and with greater frequency. Within a relatively short time, black golfers also became members of military golf teams and participated in military tournaments. A few examples are of particular interest. Murry Jacobs won an Eighth Army championship in Yokohama, Japan in late 1948. In 1952, he became the European Theater amateur champion and the following year he was crowned Seventh Army champion. In 1956, Airman Osten King fired a nine-under-par score to win the Fifth Annual Holiday-In-Dixie golf tournament at Barksdale Air Force Base in Louisiana. Clifton Harrington (together with Orville Moody and Mason Rudolph) was a member of the army golf team that won the interservice competition in 1957 at Parris Island, South Carolina. When Lee Elder was drafted into the army in 1958, he was made captain of the golf team at Fort Lewis, Washington. In 1966, Navy Petty Officer Al Mosley participated in the All-Navy Golf Tournament at Patuxent River, Maryland. Perhaps the best known of the recent group of former military golfers is Walter Morgan. He joined the Senior PGA Tour in 1991 and won his first professional event four years later.

*Another illustration of the golfing opportunities that arose when ac-
cess was no longer a problem comes from my own experiences in the military. In 1953, a mere five years after the historic desegregation order,
I was stationed as a medical officer at Fürstenfeldbruck Air Force Base
in southern Germany on the outskirts of Munich. Our family lived in
military housing just beyond the perimeter of the air base. Living next-
door were the Elmores, a white family from Oregon. Donald Elmore,
the base commissary officer, was an avid golfer. We had barely met
when Don began to insist that I take up the sport and join him on the
golf course. I acquiesced and the inevitable happened: within weeks I
became hopelessly addicted to the game and soon was the one badgering
Don to go out for a "quick nine." Had it not been for Truman's order,
I would neither have had a white neighbor nor could I have become his
playing companion on the course.*

One of the more revealing comments on present-day military attitudes is offered by a retired black Marine Corps major. He had caddied as a youngster in Houma, Louisiana, his hometown, but it was
not until he entered military service in 1961, at the age of seventeen,
that he began playing golf regularly. His game improved steadily
over the years, and by 1977 he was a scratch golfer. In 1978, he was
a member of a five-man Marine Corps golf team representing the
Hawaii area. In early 1996, I sent the former Marine Corps officer a
questionnaire that dealt with his golfing experiences while on active
duty. To a specific question regarding access to golfing facilities, he
replied, "Golf was always there for everyone and no *one* (his emphasis) in particular. Blacks looking for something to do could play golf
all day if they wanted to. The military made the game enticing at all
bases . . . I know golf was available for blacks and I remember quite a
few [African American] guys playing it and playing it well . . . "(5)

Few can deny that desegregation of the U. S. armed forces was a
big step forward in enabling blacks to learn the game of golf and to
refine their skills. It would be naive, however, to believe that all ves-
tiges of racism have been eradicated from the military golfing community. Earl Woods, a retired army lieutenant colonel and former

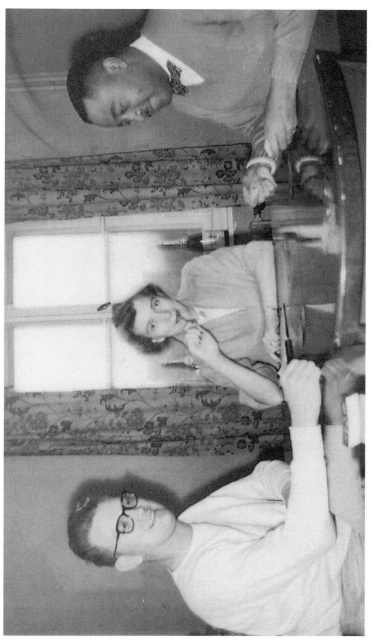

The author playing cards at the home of next-door neighbors, Donald and Joanne Elmore at the Fürstenfeldbruck Air Force Base, Germany. Circa 1954.

(Credit: Dr. Calvin Sinnette)

Green Beret, whose son Tiger has become a household name, still recalls the racial barbs to which he was subjected by some white golfers at a course on a U. S. naval base in the late 1980s. He knows that old ways die hard, and that there are some people lurking in the shadows who never learn and are beyond redemption.

When World War II ended, black golfers who had been drafted into military service began returning home eager to resume where they had left off. Many made use of their veteran's benefits to further their education while others readjusted to civilian life by returning to the workforce and raising their families. The pace of golf-related activities in the black community quickened rather remarkably in the immediate postwar period. Within a year after VJ Day, the UGA had resumed its national tournaments and the small group of black professionals lost little time getting their games into shape. A few had played while in the service, but others were less fortunate. One thing they had in common was a burning desire to prove that they were the equal of any who trod the fairways. Two fine examples of that kind of determination are found in the careers of Theodore "Ted" Rhodes and Howard "Butch" Wheeler. They dominated the black golf scene for more than a decade after the war ended, and their rivalry is one of the dramatic chapters in black golf history.

Two Postwar Black Titans of the Golf Links

Theodore "Ted" Rhodes

Among the *cognoscenti* of black golf, especially those who had the good fortune to see him during his prime, Ted Rhodes is a cult figure. Almost unanimously, they agree that he has earned a place of distinction in African American golf history. Born on November 9, 1913, in Nashville, Tennessee, Rhodes began his career in golf at age twelve when he began caddying at the Belle Meade and Richland Country Clubs in Nashville.(1) Determined to be the best golfer possible, Rhodes paid careful attention to the better players for whom he caddied. Denied the opportunity to play on any of the city's golf courses simply because he was black, Rhodes practiced in one of the city's public parks using a tree branch stuck in the ground surrounded by a circle of grass he had fashioned into a green. Over time, though, the caddiemaster at Belle Meade recognized Teddy's talent and did what he could to help him improve.

In the late 1930s, Rhodes joined the Civilian Conservation Corps before going into the Navy. Little is known about his military career except that he was stationed in Chicago and in California. At the end of World War II, he returned to Nashville for a short time before luck smiled on him in the person of heavyweight boxing champion Joe Louis. By this time an avid golfer, Louis hired Rhodes to be his personal instructor and playing partner. Shortly after he was hired, Louis sent Rhodes to California for additional training under Ray Mangrum, the brother of top professional Lloyd Mangrum. Equally important, Louis gave Rhodes the financial support he needed to play the UGA tour.

Being on the Louis payroll was mutually beneficial. Under Rhodes' tutelage, Louis improved his golfing skills considerably. For Rhodes, it meant that he no longer had to worry about finding the money to pay UGA tournament entry fees. Over the next few years, Teddy Rhodes sharpened his game and became a regular winner. In one 13-month stretch between 1946 and 1947, Rhodes won six consecutive tournaments. This string of victories was culminated by the 1947 Joe Louis Open at the Donald Ross-designed Rackham Golf Course in Detroit, where he had a score of eight-under-par 280.(2) Repeatedly, Teddy triumphed over arch rivals Howard Wheeler, Charlie Sifford, Bill Spiller, and Solomon Hughes. Although black professionals were barred from most of the major white tournaments, there were a few that allowed them to enter. Among the exceptions were the Tam O' Shanter Open in Chicago, the Los Angeles Open, and the Canadian Open. Bristling with confidence because of his success in '46 and '47, Rhodes decided to pit his skills against the nation's best.

In January of 1948, Rhodes and Bill Spiller competed in the Los Angeles Open at famed Riviera Country Club. Rhodes finished 21st and Spiller finished 34th in a field of 66 top golf professionals. On the strength of their performances at Riviera, both men automatically qualified for the next major event. Accordingly—along with Madison Gunther, a local African American amateur golfer—Rhodes and Spiller attempted to enter the Richmond (California) Open to be held January 15–18. Their entrance fees were accepted initially, but were then returned by the PGA, whose constitution at the time limited membership to Caucasians only. With Spiller's prodding, the three men sued the PGA and the Richmond club for $315,000 in damages. They charged that by being barred from the event, they were denied an opportunity to earn a living at their profession.(3) In September 1948, a few days before the case was due to open in court, the PGA pledged that it would stop preventing African American golfers from entering their tournaments (the organization's constitution still barred them from becoming PGA members). Believing that they had won the concessions they sought, the three men withdrew the suit. Rhodes returned to the black golf circuit, but not before earning a fourth place finish in the 1948 Santa Anita Open. In August 1948, one month before the PGA suit was withdrawn, Rhodes shot a four-round total of 291 at the tough Engineers Golf Course in Roslyn, Long Island to win the first Ray Robinson Open. His closest rival, Charlie Sifford, was 10 shots behind. "The huge gallery," wrote a *New York Amsterdam News* reporter," was treated to a marvelous display of golf. [Rhodes'] tee shots were straight down the middle and his irons were splitting the pins."

The former Nashville caddie had another stellar golfing year in 1949. He won the Houston Open, the Sixth City Open, the UGA national championship, the Gotham Open, the second Ray Robinson Open, and was barely edged out by Bill Spiller for a second-place finish in the Fairway Tournament held in Dayton, Ohio. In August, Rhodes was scheduled to enter the Joe Louis Invitational. On Louis' advice, though, he decided to withdraw so that he could enter a PGA tournament in Cedar Rapids, Iowa. "I told Teddy," Louis later commented," he should accept the [Iowa] invitation because it will mean more chances for Negro golfers to enter these white tournaments." One week later, however, PGA secretary George Schneiter informed Rhodes that the Cedar Rapids invitation had been sent "by mistake."(4) Rebuffed once again by PGA duplicity, Rhodes promptly entered the Joe Louis event—and won it. Later that month, Teddy's 14th-place finish in the Tam O' Shanter World Championship was the highest finish any black golfer had ever attained in the event.

At the end of the year, the sports reporter of the *Chicago De-*

fender noted: "Old Man 1949 was exceptionally good to Teddy Rhodes. The dapper little Nashvillian, with poise, power, and experience, was invincible as his dominance in golf remained supreme. The mild-mannered Teddy captured six golfing championships including the [UGA] national and the Joe Louis Invitational." The bounty of "Old Man 1949" was also seen in a different setting: in California, Rhodes married Claudia Oliver. The following year, their daughter, Deborah, was born.

Known to his many friends and admirers as "Rags" because of his fastidious dress on and off the golf course, Rhodes' golf game was characterized by accuracy off the tee, sparkling irons, and a superbly deft touch around the greens. He had a medium-brown complexion, and was about six feet tall with a lean build. Normally soft-spoken with an easygoing temperament, Teddy Rhodes was slow to anger. There was the rare occasion, however, when his temper would flare under pressure. One such incident occurred in August of 1949 at the second Ray Robinson Open at the South Shore Club on Staten Island, New York. The tournament was played during a spell of oppressive heat and was frequently interrupted by torrential downpours. Under these trying conditions, tensions mounted and there were sharp verbal exchanges during the course of play. On the second or third day Rhodes, who had been distracted repeatedly by movements and chatter nearby, asked Robinson, the main offender, to leave the golf course.(5) That Sugar Ray Robinson was the reigning welterweight boxing champion and the sponsor of the tournament meant little to Rhodes at that point. The situation had become intolerable for him, and he did not intend for his usual unflappable demeanor to be mistaken for cowardice. It is not known how the crisis was resolved but it should have been evident to all concerned that Rhodes was capable of displaying emotion when he felt badly treated.

"Rags" continued his winning ways over the next few years. In 1950, Louis Rafael Corbin, one of Joe Louis' early golf instructors, selected Rhodes as the best African American golfer of that year. The next year, Will Robinson, golf writer for the *Pittsburgh Courier* declared that Rhodes was the leading black golf professional. At the Montebello Open in southern California, his final tournament for 1951, the smooth-swinging, fashion plate from Nashville tied for fourth place.

Professional golfer Theodore "Ted" Rhodes teeing off in 1948.
(Credit: Bettmann Archives)

Early in 1952, Ted Rhodes found himself once again at the center of a controversy with the PGA. That January, he, Joe Louis, and Bill Spiller received invitations to play in the San Diego Open. Louis asked his representative, Chester Washington, to clarify the situation with Horton Smith, the newly-elected president of the PGA. At first Smith resorted to the excuse that had been used in 1948; namely, the invitations had been issued "by mistake." But this time the black golfers, anticipating another attempt at evasion, alerted the media. Under pressure, and with Spiller in an adversarial mood because he had been snubbed, Smith met with them and an agreement was reached whereby a committee would be established to formulate a list of eligible black golfers. In addition to Louis, Rhodes, and Spiller, Howard Wheeler and Eural Clark were appointed to the committee. Leonard Reed, one of Louis' staff members, served as *ex officio* advisor. Smith also obtained approval from the PGA Tournament Committee to extend invitations to eligible African American golfers for future events if the host clubs and sponsors agreed.(6)

In 1953, Rhodes won the St. Louis Public Links Invitational Open and his second Houston Open. On his way to St. Louis from Chicago in late 1953, Rhodes became ill with a reported kidney ailment. In 1954, the Burke Golf Manufacturing Company signed him to a three-year contract which enabled him to leave the Joe Louis payroll. Playing whenever and wherever he could, the dapper golf virtuoso began to lose some of his brilliance toward the end of the 1950s. Although he captured another UGA title in 1957 by defeating Charlie Sifford by three strokes, he was having increasing difficulty in putting together three or four days of championship golf. Despite the lack of consistency, he won the 1958 Gotham Open and the two-day Progressive Golf Club Tournament in Peoria, Illinois. In 1959, Rhodes lost to Cliff Harrington by one stroke at the North-South Tournament. The following year he joined a group of African American golfers to play in Havana at the invitation of the Cuban government.

Entering the 1960s, Rhodes began to realize that his health was deteriorating. He tried to continue, but by 1961 he was forced to retire. A Chicago group held a fund-raiser for him in 1962 when it was reported that he was recuperating from surgery at the Veterans Administration Hospital in Nashville. A mere shadow of his former self, "Rags" now devoted his energies to teaching. Lee Elder and Althea Gibson were two of his notable pupils.

On July 4, 1969, Theodore "Rags" Rhodes died at the El Dorado Motel in Nashville. Upon learning of his death, Lee Elder stated,

Eural Clark (left), Ted Rhodes (center) and Charlie Sifford (right) take a time out during the Phoenix Open Golf Tournament in 1952. Rhodes celebrated an opening round score of 71.   (Credit: Bettmann Archives)

"Whatever has happened to me in big-time golf and whatever success I attain eventually, I owe to Ted Rhodes."(7) Shortly after Rhodes' death, the nine-hole Cumberland Golf Course in north Nashville was renamed the Ted Rhodes Golf Course. Later that year, he was inducted posthumously into the UGA Hall of Fame. In 1993, the new 18-hole Ted Rhodes Golf Course was opened to the public. In 1998, the Tennessee Golf Foundation will induct

Theodore Rhodes into its Hall of Fame. He will be the only inductee of the year. These honors, late in coming, are fitting tributes to one of the most outstanding golfers born in the United States; someone who never achieved his full potential because of a nation's inability to move beyond the moral and intellectual bankruptcy of racial discrimination.

Howard "Butch" Wheeler

Tall as one of the pine trees for which his home state is renowned, and possessing an unorthodox cross-handed grip, Howard Wheeler was one of the longest drivers of a golf ball during the 1930s and 1940s. Rapidly coiling and uncoiling his willowy frame, his body acted as a powerful sling that enabled him to generate tremendous clubhead speed. Born in Atlanta, Georgia, on April 8, 1911, he was one of six children in the Wheeler family.(8) He completed elementary school in Atlanta before he began caddying at local country clubs. He was one of Bobby Jones' favorite caddies at the Brookhaven Country Club, and eventually became caddiemaster at East Lake Country Club.

His first tournament win was the 1931 Atlanta Open. It was also the first event he had entered as a professional. In 1933, he defeated John Brooks Dendy of Ashville, North Carolina, to win the Southern Open. On the second day of the tournament, held at Lincoln Country Club, Wheeler shot a 62. Upon completion of the event, J.C. Chunn, a reporter for the *Pittsburgh Courier*, dubbed him "Atlanta's Man of Destiny." Later that year in Kankakee, Illinois, he won the first of his six UGA national championships.

"Butch" Wheeler won his second UGA championship in 1938 and his victory was reported by *Time* magazine. Unfortunately, the article was written in the patronizing style that was all too familiar to generations of black golfers. Describing the tournament, the article read in part:

> After the first round, however, the greater part of the gallery of 300 trudged around after lanky, wooly-topped Howard Wheeler of Atlanta—watched him tee up on the edge of a match folder, shuffle along the fairways in a Stepin Fetchit gait,

plop down on the greens while waiting his turn to putt . . . .
With a minimum of effort, he got results that would please
many a topflight white golfer; rounds of 68, 73, 72, 71—on a
tough, hilly course he had never seen before. His 284 not only
won the tournament and the first prize of $200 but set a new
record for the Negro championship - just three strokes higher
than the all-time U. S. Open record set by Ralph Guldahl last
year. With this accomplishment, Howard Wheeler took his
place alongside Bobby Jones, Charley Yates and others who
have made Atlanta a starred spot on the golfing map.(9)

A few days after winning the UGA championship, Wheeler
teamed with Frank Radcliff of New York to defeat two white golfers,

*Long-hitting Howard "Butch"
Wheeler won six times in the
professional division of the UGA
National Championships. Circa 1937.*

Charles Havlacek and Gene Battis-
toni. On his way to that victory at
the Palos Park Golf Course in
Chicago, Wheeler shot a course
record of 65. It was a feat to please
any topflight golfer. Three years
later, Wheeler won another interra-
cial match. This time paired with
Clyde Martin—Joe Louis' professional instructor—the two-man
team defeated Chuck Kocsis, a former Walker Cup player, and his
brother, Emerick, the reigning
Michigan PGA champion.(10)

Despite his excellent play,
Wheeler could not sustain himself
purely on earnings from golf. To
make ends meet he had to find
other sources of income. Although
the dates are uncertain, in the late
1930s Wheeler met Eddie Mallory,
a small-time band leader and golf
devotee. At the time, Mallory was
married to the popular entertainer
Ethel Waters. A dandy with expen-

sive tastes and a lust for life in the fast lane, Mallory was once described by a reporter for the *Chicago Defender* as someone who "In addition to setting the pace of the best dressed man in America . . . is an ardent golf enthusiast having attained the coveted ranks, via the trophy route, of amateur pro (sic) . . . .Unlike his famous wife, he does not go in for riding along the bridle path. He much prefers to go in for accurate putts or drives . . ."

Aware of Wheeler's precarious financial situation, Mallory offered Atlanta's "Man of Destiny" a job as his wife's chauffeur. Wheeler readily accepted and, for a number of months thereafter, he was seen driving Miss Waters around metropolitan New York. On one occasion he drove the entertainer from New York City to a performing engagement at Shady Rest Golf & Country Club in New Jersey. Wheeler used the opportunity to play a round of golf. In February 1938, Wheeler was involved in an automobile accident while driving Waters and her husband in a blinding snowstorm outside Boston. Fortunately, the occupants escaped without injury but the three vehicles involved in the accident were severely damaged.(11) After a relatively short period, Wheeler's financial situation became less vulnerable and he moved to California.

With Los Angeles as his new home, "Butch" Wheeler played in a number of tournaments including the 1942 Tam O' Shanter Open. In one account of that event, it was reported that Wheeler blistered one of his drives over 300 yards. A few newspapermen who missed the shot asked him to repeat the effort. The tall Georgian, "mounted his ball on the matchbox he was using for a tee and did the shot over again, distance and all . . ." Although he could delight the galleries with his prodigious drives, he seemed unable to play with the consistency that was required to post low scores. In the midst of his unhappiness, the army beckoned and Wheeler went off to war. In a way, it was a golf blessing in disguise.

When he returned from military service, Wheeler quickly regained much of his old prowess. He defeated Ted Rhodes for the 1946 UGA national championship, and won it again in '47 and '48. In 1951, he won the Joe Louis Invitational at Rackham Golf Course in Detroit, defeating Al Besselink, the defending champion. One indication of the level of play was the order of finish at the end of the tournament. Wheeler was number one, Besselink number two, Ted

Rhodes number three, Charlie Sifford number four, and Bill Spiller number five.(12)

After moving to Philadelphia, Wheeler remained competitive until 1958 when he registered his last UGA championship at the North Park Golf Course in Pittsburgh. Following this, his sixth UGA triumph, he began having difficulty with arthritis. In 1963 he was inducted into the UGA Hall of Fame. Though increasingly incapacitated by illness, the former Georgia caddie stayed active in Philadelphia golf matters. On April 25, 1968, while attending a meeting of the Fairview Golf Club Tournament Committee in Philadelphia, he collapsed and died within minutes.

One of the truly important black golfers in the history of the game in the United States, Howard Wheeler never made any serious attempts to play in PGA-sponsored tournaments. Nevertheless, his easygoing manner and homespun brand of wry humor belied a fierce sense of pride. In a 1951 newspaper article, Wheeler revealed his sense of self-worth and quiet dignity:

> "Wheeler was sitting in the locker room tying his shoes one day when he heard a man ask, 'Well, how'd you do today, boy?' Wheeler just kept tying his shoes. The man tugged at his sleeve then, 'I said, how'd you do today, boy?' he repeated. Wheeler looked up unsmiling, 'Just fine Mister', he replied.
>
> The man smiled and walked away. Suddenly he turned on his heels to where Wheeler sat. He cleared his throat and said, 'I didn't mean it that way.'
>
> 'Mean what, what way?' Wheeler inquired blandly.
>
> 'Well,' the man said uncertainly,' I asked how did you do today, Boy and you said, 'Just fine, Mister.' 'I didn't mean 'Boy' the way you thought.
>
> 'Oh, that's O. K.' Wheeler assured him. 'I guess it just depends on how you were brought up. Now my folks told me when I was a boy that when you don't know a man's name, it's proper to call him 'Mister.' Yep it's all in the way you were brought up."(13)

Long before Howard "Butch" Wheeler mastered the skills of golf, he had been taught the importance of respect and courtesy.

The pent-up desires of returning servicemen to fulfill their old or newly-found golfing aspirations were evident in the torrent of related activities that were unleashed. New golf courses began to spring up in all parts of the country, golf equipment sales mushroomed, professional and amateur golf events increased in number, publication of golf instructional material soared, and the burgeoning golfing public eagerly sought all available means to satisfy the requirements of their favorite game.

And that included black *women* golfers as well.

7 | The Struggle Within a Struggle

Aphotograph in the collection of the Library of Congress in Washington, D.C. provides an indication of early African American female association with the game of golf. Taken around 1905, the photograph shows a young black girl about ten years old addressing what appears to be a golf ball with a makeshift golf club. In the photo as well are two young black onlookers also holding golf clubs.(1) The place where the photograph was taken is not known. In 1909, *American Golfer* magazine carried a photograph of a somewhat older black female holding what appears to be a wood-shafted iron in a semiaddress position. A third item pertaining to the early association of African American women with golf appeared in a December 1914 issue of the newspaper *Western Outlook*. Described at one time in its lengthy masthead as "A Journal Devoted To The Interests Of The Negro On The Pacific Coast And The Betterment Of His Condition," the newspaper printed a short instructional article entitled, "Hints on Golf for Women." Somewhat patronizingly, the article commented, "There is another point that women players, even experienced ones, are apt to neglect, and that is the rules of the game." Whoever wrote the article advised golfers to buy a book of rules ". . . so there is no excuse for any one being in a state of ignorance." There was no explanatory text accompanying either of the photographs and no indication in the newspaper article that women were golfing in increasing numbers. Nevertheless, when considered collectively, these three items at least *suggest* that golf held a certain

Black children with makeshift golf clubs. Circa 1905.
(Credit: Library of Congress)

degree of interest for African American women in the early years of the twentieth century.

In the 1920s, early black golf writer E.L. Renip observed that golf " . . . is indeed the old man's game and the old woman's game, too, for that matter."(2) Later in the same decade, photographs appeared in African American newspapers showing black women holding golf clubs. In one of these photographs, Mrs. Harry Wills, wife of the New Orleans-born heavyweight boxer, was shown holding what appeared to be a driver while bedecked in a dome-shaped hat, shirtwaist dress, and high-heeled shoes. Once again, unfortunately, neither the photo's caption nor the accompanying story gave any indication why Mrs. Wills posed with a golf club.

For scholars of the period, the March 1925 issue of the magazine *Survey Graphic* is considered to be "a landmark in black literature."(3) It was a publication that appeared during that period of remarkable creative activity later referred to as the Negro or Harlem Renaissance. One of the articles in the issue was written by Elise Johnson McDougald, a newly-appointed assistant principal in a Harlem elementary school. Entitled "The Double Task: The Struggle Of Negro Women For Sex And Race Emancipation," McDougald classified black women into groups based on their activities. The first she described as " . . . a very small leisure group - the wives and daughters of men who are in business, in the professions and in a few well-paid personal service occupations." A member herself of that privileged first group, McDougald indicated with obvious pride that in their " . . . homes of comparative ease . . . we find the polite activities of social exclusiveness." This group had the "luxuries of well-appointed homes, modest motors, tennis, golf and country clubs, trips to Europe and California."

In the lengthy article, McDougald argued forcefully against gender differentials and against the negative stereotypes of black women, "having lower sex standards." While she pleaded for sympathy and assistance for black single mothers, she denied that the moral values of black working-class mothers differed from those of other ethnic groups. Her vision of black motherhood, nevertheless, was a product of the generation into which she was born. Undoubtedly she intended otherwise, but the classification of African American women according to the system devised by the well-meaning Harlem school teacher tended to reinforce the image of golf as a symbol for elitism and genteel snobbery. Even though it may have been interpreted less severely in the 1920s, it is difficult to believe that McDougald's article helped to generate enthusiasm for the game among less-financially-well-off black women.

It was not until the end of the decade that black women appeared consistently as serious golfers in African American newspapers. In 1930, black women entered the UGA national championship tournament for the first time. The winner that year was Marie Thompson of Chicago, Illinois, and the runner-up was Lucy Williams of Indianapolis, Indiana. The two finished in the same order the following year, but Williams turned the tables on her rival in 1932 to reverse the order of finish. Over the 10-year period from 1930 to 1940, Williams was UGA national women's champion three times and the runner-up on five occasions.

In addition to their entrance onto the national golf scene, other events occurred to make the 1930s a momentous decade for African American women golfers. On April 22, 1937, Wake-Robin Golf Club, the first formal organization of African American women golfers was founded in Washington, D. C. Helen Webb Harris convened a meeting of 13 women at her "R" Street home in the northwest section of the city. On hand to assist were six members of the all-male Royal Golf Club. For years the women had endured the scorn of many of their "menfolk" and decided the time had come to form an autonomous body. They had sought to become an auxiliary of the Royal Golf Club but they were rejected. Yet, at the initial meeting, six 'defectors' from the Royals were present to do what they could to help the women get their own organization started. Among them was Dr. Albert Harris, husband of the convener, and Herbert Bethea, who later not only gave instructions to neophyte Wake-Robin golfers, but also donated the trophy for the first annual Wake-Robin golf tournament. By the end of the meeting, Helen Harris was elected president; Adelaide Adams, vice-president; Dorothy Brown, financial secretary; Evelyn Beam, recording secretary; Mabel Jones, club instructor; Vydie Carter, reporter; and Ethel Williams, chaplain. (A wake-robin is a short, purple and yellow wildflower that grows plentifully in the mid-Atlantic region of the United States. It is also referred to as a Jack-in-the-pulpit).

Formation of the Wake-Robin Golf Club was much more than the getting together of a group of nice little black ladies to play golf on a regular basis. In 1987, at the time of the club's 50th anniversary, one observer noted: "Under a system of racism, in an atmosphere of sexism, black women playing golf was not a light matter. It was a political act."(4) An incident which occurred one year after the club came into existence demonstrated the political consciousness of the founding members. To celebrate its first anniversary, Wake-Robin held a banquet at a well-known local restaurant. Once again supporting members of the Royal Golf Club were in attendance. Wake-Robin used the occasion to add its voice to those demanding a golf course for the black community. "A committee representing both clubs was appointed to call on the Secretary of the Interior and place directly before him the conditions under which golfers are forced to play in Washington and to outline a future program."(5) Out of these continuing efforts, the nine-hole Langston Golf Course was opened in 1939. In 1941, as a result of continuing dialogue between Wake-Robin and the Department of Interior, Secretary Harold Ickes ordered Washington, D. C. public golf courses desegregated.

In its more than 60-year history, Wake-Robin Golf Club has a long list of achievements on which it can look back with pride. Each year it has held a club tournament; during World War II, it raised funds to purchase medical equipment for the armed forces; it established a junior golf program; it witnessed four of its members elected to the UGA Hall of Fame; and it has watched its membership (active and honorary) more than quadruple. Most importantly, Wake-Robin led the way for other African American women golfers across the country to form independent golf organizations.

In November of 1937, a mere seven months after the formation of Wake-Robin, Anna Mae Robinson led a group of black women golfers in Chicago to establish the Chicago Women's Golf Club (CWGC). Robinson was elected its first president. Just as there was a small reservoir of enlightened males who assisted Wake-Robin in its formation, the venerable Walter Speedy played a similar role in the founding of the CWGC. Because of the assistance he provided, the women of the Chicago group referred to Speedy as "father of the organization," and his wife, Nettie, as "mother of the organization."(6) Facing conditions that paralleled those of other black female golfers across the country, the newly-formed CWGC decided to embark on a militant course of action. In 1939, it sent two delegates—Robinson and Ella M. Williams—to the UGA's national meeting in Los Angeles. "Our mission was to request membership in the all-male golfing association," related Robinson in a 1973 interview. "This was something completely new. The men didn't like the idea. Some of the men thought we would try to take over. But we outnumbered them." With great pride Robinson recalled that "We were the first women to join UGA." Now energized by success, the Chicago group of women hosted the annual UGA tournament in 1940. Geneva Wilson and Elizabeth Mitchell of Chicago, and Rhoda Fowler of New York, served on the championship committee. In 1941, Paris Brown, then president of Wake-Robin, was elected vice-president of the UGA. Within a two-year stretch, black women

Rhoda Fowler of New York City was a pioneering black woman golfer and a former Women's Eastern Champion. Circa 1935.

golfers had made notable forward strides in the organizational structure of black golf.

Obviously capable of handling themselves with distinction in the "political" arena, black women also proved to some of their male detractors that they were equally capable of playing the game with skill. By 1941, when golfing activities were curtailed by World War II, a pool of talented black women golfers had emerged to provide ample proof that gender-based claims of female athletic inferiority were sheer nonsense. On the West Coast there was Martha Clisby of Pasadena, California and (Mrs.) Emmanuel Joseph of Oakland, California. In the South there was Roberta Holland of Jacksonville, Florida; Thelma McTyre and her sister Theresa Howell of Atlanta, Georgia; and (Mrs.) Cleveland Abbott from Tuskegee, Alabama. Top-notch midwestern golfers were Lucy Williams and Ella Able of Indianapolis, Indiana; Julia Siler of St. Louis, Missouri; and Cleo Ball and Geneva Wilson from Chicago. The East Coast provided Laura Thoroughgood and Rhoda Fowler of New York City. The invitation extended to Geneva Wilson to play in the 1944 Tam O' Shanter tournament in Chicago marked the first time an African American woman golfer participated in a major national event. It was a clear indication that competent black women golfers could compete with the best.(7)

Over the next two years, black women golfers made continued progress in the quest for parity with their male counterparts. In 1947, however, an incident occurred indicating that male chauvinism was alive and well. At the third Joe Louis Open in 1946, women golfers were involved in a series of disputes. The exact nature of the disputes is not known nor is it known how the disputes were handled. The problem persisted, obviously, because in May of 1947, Bernard O'Dell, director of the Joe Louis tournament, announced rather imperiously:

> " . . . .women will not be permitted to compete in the tournament this year. Last year the bars were lowered and the gals were granted the privilege of competing, but several disputes centered around women competitors and the committee turned them down this year.
>
> One particular instance that caused the committee to frown on the gals was the disturbance created by a woman who denounced the prize she was given." (8)

Over the next two months, O'Dell was deluged with complaints from women who had been barred from participating in the event. In the majority, the women argued reasonably that, "the tournament committee should bar the several women who caused the trouble, and not the entire group."

Once again it is not known how the matter was resolved, if at all. Two years later, charges and countercharges were still being made. "The girls have complained loud and long against certain restrictions," wrote Thelma McTyre in a *Chicago Defender* column, "particularly those which prevent us from entering a number of tournaments." The issue had been raised at the UGA annual winter meeting in February of 1949 and, in language painfully similar to the shallow PGA response made years later when questioned about its "Caucasians only" policy, then-president A. D. V. Crosby explained "While UGA could not compel club members to open their tournaments to women golfers, UGA could urge them to lift all restrictions against the girls."

Women members of the UGA also resented their exclusion from leadership positions in the organization. Even though a Wake-Robin representative had been elected vice-president in 1941, she was a rare exception. With the resumption of normal activities after the end of World War II, the issue of female membership on the executive committee finally came to a head at the 1949 annual meeting. After a heated floor debate, Catherine Dixon was elected assistant secretary and it enabled her to become a member of the executive body. Earlier in the meeting, Dixon was quoted by McTyre as asking, "We women want to know if there is a rule which prevents us from playing in some tournaments, and if there is no [such] rule, why are we barred?"(9)

Another good question concerned the military. Desegregation of the armed forces had not proved to be as helpful to African American women golfers as it had been to their male counterparts. Few black female military personnel had been attracted to the sport despite the relative accessibility of golf courses where they could play. Consequently, none emerged from the ranks of the military as serious golfing prospects. Lucy Bond, a retired army lieutenant colonel who spent 20 years in the service, encountered few black women on military golf courses during her career. After her retirement, Bond joined the International Women Veterans Golf Association. Its members, including a few British and Canadian women, served in all branches of the armed services. Over the years, Bond does not recall meeting any other black members.(10)

Many significant events in the evolution of black women's golf occurred after the end of World War II. First and foremost was the sizeable increase in the numbers of black women golfers and their organizations. Slowly, black women golfers began to appear with greater frequency on the nation's golf courses. The organized groups were more assertive in the UGA, they sponsored their own golf tournaments, and were particularly active in sponsoring junior golf. During this period, two black women emerged who made notable contributions to the game. Not surprisingly, Ann Gregory of Gary, Indiana and Paris Brown of Washington D.C. are names that are relatively unfamiliar to the golfing public. Referred to, respectively, as the "Queen of Negro Golf Women" and "The First Lady of Black Golf," Gregory and Brown were exemplars of the finest attributes in golf. They justly deserve recognition for their outstanding legacies.

Ann Gregory

The middle child of five, Ann Moore was born to Myra and Henry Moore in Aberdeen, Mississippi, on July 25, 1912. When Ann was about fifteen her father died. Her mother died shortly afterward, and the five children were parceled out among relatives. Ann lived briefly with an older married sister and her husband before accepting employment as the live-in maid for the Sanders, a white Aberdeen family. With her engaging personality and responsible attitude, Ann soon endeared herself to the family, who saw to it that she finished high school.

In 1930, to the sorrow of the Sanders, Ann followed her married sister when she moved to Gary, Indiana. Naturally athletic, Ann began playing tennis. Her skills with the racquet improved to the extent that she won the Gary city championship in 1937. The following year, she married Leroy Percy Gregory (often referred to as Percy by relatives and friends), an employee in the coke factory of the United States Steel Corporation in Gary. Leroy Gregory was a longtime golfer who played whenever the opportunity presented itself. Their only child, JoAnn, was born in 1942 and, less than a year later, Leroy was drafted for service in the United States Navy where he remained until his discharge in 1945.(11)

After their marriage, Leroy's golf playing became increasingly irksome to his new bride. Night after night she watched her husband eat cold suppers that she had labored to prepare earlier in the day. In one newspaper account, she recalled, "He came home late nearly every day, telling me that he was at the golf course. I couldn't believe somebody would spend that much time chasing a little white ball." Ann's annoyance with her husband's golfing activities grew steadily worse until she began contemplating divorce. As she neared the limits of her tolerance, World War II intervened and Leroy had to abandon his golf clubs for military service. With her husband away, Ann realized that even though Leroy's golf was a source of irritation, she missed him terribly. One day not long after Leroy's departure, Ann dressed herself in sports attire, grabbed her husband's clubs, got in the family automobile and headed for the golf course. The game's appeal was almost instantaneous, and Ann succumbed to the lure of golf. For the remainder of her husband's military service, Ann played regularly. Never again did she doubt Leroy's reasons for coming home late for supper after a round of golf.

Soon after she began playing, Ann's potential caught the attention of Calvin Ingraham, a teaching professional from Chicago. With Ingraham's coaching, Ann's game improved considerably. When Leroy returned home in 1945, he discovered that his wife had become an accomplished golfer. In late July of that year, Ann entered the eighth annual CWGC midwest golf tournament and was runner-up to Geneva Lumpkin in the second flight.(12) Ann and Leroy played together at least two to three times a week over the next four or five years. In July of 1948, each of them was a winner in their respective events in a tournament in Kankakee, Illinois. Over the three-day event, Ann defeated Lucy Mitchell, Cleo Ball, and Geneva Wilson, all of whom were former UGA national women's champions. The victory provided an all-expenses-paid trip to that year's national tournament. Unfortunately, there is no record of how she fared in the national event. Twelve months later, at the site of that same tournament, Ann posted a sparkling 71 during a friendly round.

In July of 1950, *Chicago Defender* golf writer Russ Cowans expressed disappointment at the small number of young black women golfers. He observed that Ann was among a group of older women who " . . . have reached the zenith of their career and are on the way down the hill."(13) It is not known if Ann Gregory read the column, but her performance throughout 1950 decisively refuted Cowans' predictions. In late July, she was victorious in the Sixth City Open held in Cleveland, Ohio. She then went on to win the Midwest Amateur in early August, and later equaled the women's course record at a Flint, Michigan tournament. Ann capped the 1950 season by defeating the highly respected Eoline Thornton, 5 and 3, to capture the women's title at the national UGA tournament in Washington, D. C. Obviously contrite about what he had written earlier that year, Russ Cowans' newspaper column at the end of 1950 was almost apologetic. "Is Ann Gregory," he asked, "the greatest of Negro women golfers? That's one of the questions golfers have been asking since the Gary, Ind. housewife captured six championships in the seven tournaments she played this year. This achievement surpasses the efforts of such previous champions as Cleo Ball, Lucy Mitchell, Thelma Cowans, and Mary Brown. None of them dominated the field as Ann did this year." Concluding the column, Cowans remarked: "Experts who have been watching Ann maintain that she's the best Negro woman golfer to come along, and that she should be able to beat back all challengers for the next two or three years."(14)

Over the next half-decade—invariably accompanied by her husband-coach and confidant, Leroy, and her daughter JoAnn—Ann Gregory was such a dominant force in African American women's golf that on at least one occasion, because of her huge margins of victory, some of her competitors asked for handicaps. She collected so many trophies that a 1953 publication noted she and Leroy were compelled to build an addition to their home at 2428 Madison Street in Gary. The additional space, of course, provided only temporary relief. In 1952, 1953, and 1954, Ann continued to accumulate awards with monotonous regularity. In 1953, she won the CWGC tournament; in 1954, victory came in the eighth annual Minnesota Open; in 1955 she defeated Theresa Howell, Hazel Bibbs, and Alice Stewart to win the fifth annual Vehicle City Open in Flint, Michigan.

One of the most memorable moments in Ann Gregory's stellar golfing career occurred in 1956. By this time it was apparent to Ann that she would be unable to raise her golfing ability to the level she desired if she confined herself to the black women's golfing circuit.

She discussed the situation with members of the CWGC, which she had joined in 1952, and it was decided that the organization should apply for affiliated membership in the United States Golf Association (USGA) so that Ann could be eligible to enter their events. CWGC's application was approved and it became USGA's first black member club. As a result, Ann Gregory became the first African American woman golfer to enter a USGA-sponsored event—the U.S. Women's Amateur. On September 17, 1956, at the Meridian Hills Country Club in Indianapolis, she teed off in the opening round against Carolyn Cudone but lost to her opponent 2 and 1. Although she had qualified to play in the Tam O' Shanter tournament as early as 1947, Ann needed regular exposure to the nation's better golfers. Participation in the 1956 USGA event marked the beginning of her competition in national championships. She continued for more than 30 years.

Throughout the 1960s and 1970s, Ann maintained her mastery over other black women golfers. From all indications, she won more than 100 golfing events during the 20-year span. In addition to victories in many parts of the continental United States, the "Queen of Negro Golf Women" scored triumphs in Spain, Hawaii, Puerto Rico, and the Bahamas. On some of these occasions she played with guest celebrities Joe Louis, Althea Gibson, and Jackie Robinson.(15) It was also the period in which she became better known on the USGA's women's amateur circuit. Although Eoline Thornton, Althea Gibson, and Renee Powell had competed in some of the major white tournaments in the late 1950s and late 1960s, it was Ann who appeared more frequently at national events. But in the process she suffered her share of indignities. Even before venturing onto the national circuit in the early 1960s, Ann confronted bigoted officials at the Gleason Park public golf course in Gary. Until that time, African American golfers were confined to a nine-hole course while white golfers enjoyed access to the eighteen-hole layout. Demanding the right to play where she chose, Ann paid her fee and strode to the first tee of the larger course. She played the round without interference and through her resolute action, the Gleason Park officials abandoned their racial double standards.

Other incidents followed. In 1959, Ann was denied entry into the players' banquet at Congressional Country Club in Bethesda, Mary-

Ann Gregory, the first black woman to enter a USGA event,
posing with a trophy awarded in 1967.
(Credit: Mrs. JoAnn Overstreet)

land, at the conclusion of the U.S. Women's Amateur. In 1963, she was mistaken for a maid by another contestant at the Women's Amateur in Williamstown, Massachusetts. The 1959 episode was doubly painful for Ann. The Bethesda event was held at the same time as the UGA national tournament in neighboring Washington, D. C. When Ann decided to forego the UGA event to compete at Congressional, some black golfers accused her of deserting the UGA in favor of the white organization.(16) It was a classic "no win" situation in which an African American is thrust into the impossible position of trying to reconcile the chance to enhance self-development with what some perceive as group solidarity. On the horns of this dilemma, Ann was compelled to accept one of two equally attractive opportunities and reject the other. Unfortunately, her decision led to an unfavorable outcome where the absurdities of race prevented reason from prevailing. The dissatisfaction expressed by the small group of black golfers was short-lived, however, and wiser heads in the UGA were convinced that her actions were not intended to thwart or jeopardize the goals and objectives of the organization.

Virtually invincible in her prime, Gregory was often approached to turn professional. Ann steadfastly refused. In 1950, she commented: "My main thought is my little girl. I want her to be a fine pianist and I'm working hard toward that end. I will not let golf get between me and my family, although I love the game."(17) Nor did she permit love of the game to interfere with her numerous community and civic activities. She was the first African American trustee of the Gary Public Library Board and was later elected its president. She was also a member of the executive board of the local United Fund Campaign and a member of the advisory board of St. Mary's Mercy Medical Center. An ardent churchgoer, Ann was an active choir member at a local Methodist church.

Slightly under 5'10" and weighing about 165 pounds, Ann was a stylish, sophisticated dresser with a commanding but not overbearing presence. She enjoyed the challenge of leadership positions and held many elected offices in the CWGC, including the presidency. She also served as its first tournament director. As someone who felt keenly about giving something back to the game, she frequently conducted golf clinics for both juniors and adults. In recognition of her contributions to golf, the UGA inducted Ann into its Hall of Fame in 1966.

By 1980, Ann's playing schedule consisted mainly of USGA senior events. In 1981, she won the 65-and-up division at a tournament in Spring Lake Heights, New Jersey and placed 18th overall among 100 competitors.(18) On that occasion, a USGA official remarked, "She's just the most dominant player over 65 in the country."

About this time, Leroy began to ail. He had been injured while in the Navy during World War II, and as he grew older the effects of the injury began to take their toll. He withstood a number of operations, but then developed Alzheimer's disease. He lingered for another four years and died in May of 1989.

Relying on golf to help her cope with the loss of her beloved Leroy, Ann entered the U. S. National Senior Olympics in June of that year. After struggling through the early holes, she went on to beat a field of 50 women and set a Senior Olympics record. The gold medal worn at the end of the long red, white, and blue ribbon around her neck was perhaps the most cherished of her more than 400 trophies and awards. "This gold medal," said Ann in an interview shortly after the event, "is a tribute to my Leroy. If I could only have him home once more to see this medal."(19) In late 1989, Ann played in a tournament in Sea Island, Georgia, during which she developed a stubborn respiratory infection. Although she managed to travel to Alaska to spend Christmas with her daughter, son-in-law, and two grandchildren, she never completely recovered from the infection. A few days after returning to Gary in late January, her condition worsened. By the time she was taken to the hospital, she was beyond assistance. Ann Moore Gregory died on February 5, 1990 and was buried in Gary.

In his book *A Hard Road to Glory*, the late tennis star Arthur Ashe noted, " . . . many observers hailed Ann Gregory as the best black woman golfer ever." The record indicates that no one else even came close.

A granite marker, erected in the summer of 1996 to her memory, stands at the sixth hole of the South Gleason Park Golf Course in Gary.

Paris Brown

The youngest of Lewis and Lula Toomer's 10 children, Paris Bernice Toomer was born on November 15, 1901 in Byron, Georgia. After completing elementary school in her hometown, she went to the Cooke Normal School in St. Louis, Missouri. There she completed her education and became an elementary school teacher. In 1925, she met her husband-to-be, Edgar Brown, who had moved to St. Louis from Sandoval, Illinois in late adolescence. Brown, a militant civil rights activist throughout his life, was an all-around athlete and excellent tennis player.(20) In 1927, Paris and Edgar married, and within a year their first son, Edward, was born.

Edgar Brown lost his job in St. Louis soon after the 1929 stock market crash. Leaving his family behind, he went to Chicago in search of employment. Fortunately, he met with success fairly quickly and was able to send for his wife and child. Though busy with her household responsibilities, Paris managed to find a few spare moments for recreation. Someone introduced her to golf and it captured her interest immediately. Due to her husband's encouragement, and his playing companionship on the golf course, Paris played as frequently as possible.

Shortly after the presidential elections of 1932, Edgar Brown obtained a civil service job in Washington, D. C. The family was separated once again, but were reunited within a few months. In 1933, a second son, Frederick, was born. It left Paris very little free time. As the children grew, however, Paris gradually resumed her golfing pastime. She also obtained part-time employment as a census taker. In late 1937, at its second meeting, Paris joined the Wake-Robin Golf Club.

It did not take long for the membership to recognize her strong leadership qualities; within two years she was elected the organization's second president. Because of her new position she was selected to be Wake-Robin's delegate to the UGA. In 1941, while attending an annual UGA meeting in Boston, Massachusetts, Paris was elected vice-president and became the first woman to hold an executive position in the organization's 15-year history. Around this same time, she volunteered to serve on the tournament committee. A few years later, she was appointed assistant tournament director with responsibility for managing women's events. Her administrative and organizational skills soon attracted attention. In 1954, despite the opposition of some male members, Paris B. Brown was elected to the position of UGA tournament director. It was another first in her illustrious golfing career.

In her prime, Paris Brown was a stylish woman with a stately bearing. She had a low-pitched voice, deliberate speech, and was characterized as someone "with the patience of Job and the wisdom of Solomon."(21) Under the most trying of circumstances, she maintained an unflappable demeanor. At the height of her tenure, the annual UGA tournaments sometimes attracted upwards of 400 players. Working for weeks at a stretch before the event, and with a minimum of resources at her command, Paris took care of the minutest details to ensure that conditions of play were as close to optimal as humanly possible. One of her early innovations was to arrange for the installation of a public address system by the first tee so that individual players and their affiliations could be announced to the assembled gallery. Initiated on an experimental basis for the amateur flights, the new procedure proved so popular that the professionals began to clamor for the new feature to be added to their division as well. To friends and foes alike, it was evident that the former Wake-Robin president was a creative and highly competent tournament director.

More than anything else, Paris was noted for impartial and reasoned judgment. It was immaterial if someone was a scratch golfer or a high handicapper, an amateur or a professional, a celebrity or an unknown. Her decisions were based strictly and solely on the official rules. Her antipathy to betting on tournament play was legendary, and the surest way for a player to be disqualified was to be caught placing a bet. Yet, despite her unyielding adherence to rules, "Ma" Brown, as she was affectionately known, was held in high esteem.

The tall, bespectacled woman to whom "golf was her life," traveled widely to improve opportunities for black golfers and to encourage African American women to play the game.(22) Paris Brown firmly believed that one day African Americans would prove beyond the slightest doubt that they could master the game. She felt, therefore, that it was essential to establish the highest standards for governing play and conduct at all UGA tournaments. Accordingly, tournament schedules became noted for having a well-defined order of events based on punctuality, courtesy, and decorum. Time and time again, "Ma" Brown took what had been a haphazard, ill-managed event and turned it into a well-run, disciplined operation. Still, she was always prepared to listen to the opinions of others. She did not draw hasty conclusions, nor did she display any hint of omniscience or arrogance. Through tact and gentle persuasion, she defused many heated disputes. Her personal conduct during these situations was always above reproach.

In order to express the seriousness with which she took her responsibilities, Paris developed a statement of principles that was distributed to UGA-affiliated organizations in 1959. Excerpts from the statement include:

- Make certain of your golf course.
- The Tournament Committee should send out all players and not let golfers make up [their] own foursomes. This gives the picture of the lack of proper direction.
- Avoid favoritism. You cannot favor your friends without hurting many others, thereby making enemies for all times.
- Stick to the rules - sometimes it will be hard but you win the respect of your fellow golfers.
- See that each member of your club has a rule book and knows the rules of the game.
- The Tournament Committee should have on hand at all times a Rule Book. If a matter comes up for interpretation, the Committee, with the person or persons involved, should read the rule together. Never attempt to quote a rule; it is much safer to read it, then [there is] no chance for a misquote. NOTE: While looking up the rule, it gives the player an opportunity to "cool off."
- Never make a decision without hearing all sides of the question. After the committee has so ruled, DO NOT CHANGE.
- Golf is a game for ladies and gentlemen. It calls for honesty and good sportsmanship. If you abide by the rules of the game, your conscience will never disturb you.(23)

Paris not only promoted the annual UGA tournaments tirelessly and selfishly, she was at the forefront of organizational efforts aimed at encouraging young African Americans to play golf and to possibly parlay their fairway skills into avenues for furthering their education. She was someone who symbolized honesty and integrity, but was neither aloof nor prudish. On the contrary, she was a gregarious and gracious person who enjoyed sporting events, parties, and church activities. Even though gambling at golf was anathema to her, she was not opposed to indulging in games of chance in a social setting. Following meetings of the Wake-Robin club, she frequently joined other members for a poker session. At the end of the club season, it was not uncommon for her to invite a group of members and guests to her summer cottage on Maryland's eastern shore for a fish fry.

In recognition of her outstanding efforts on behalf of black golf, Paris B. Brown was inducted into the UGA Hall of Fame in 1963. Unfortunately, despite her notable achievements and superb leadership qualities—or perhaps because of them—there were a few UGA members (predominantly male) who envied her success and widespread admiration. Campaigning relentlessly for her ouster, they eventually succeeded in making it happen. In 1964, more in sorrow than anger, Paris Brown resigned as UGA tournament director. Always taking the high road, however, she continued to serve on the tournament committee for many years thereafter. Timothy Thomas, a long-time golfer in the metropolitan Washington, D. C. area, succeeded Paris Brown as tournament director. He consulted with her frequently after his appointment, and she was always willing to assist. On January 15, 1977, in the presence of a large audience, the Eastern Golf Association held a testimonial dinner for "Ma" Brown. Typical of the sentiments that were expressed that evening were the words in Charlie Sifford's telegram stating: "You have given so much to golf." Paris also received a letter from former PGA Commissioner Joseph C. Dey, Jr., who wrote " . . . to congratulate [you] on all the good and constructive things you have done for golf these many years."

Paris Brown remained active in the Wake-Robin Golf Club during the later years of her life. She was also involved in church activities and volunteered her services for special education programs in the Washington, D. C. public school system. On October 20, 1990 after ailing for a number of years, "the first lady of Black golf" died in the nation's capital at the age of 88. Befittingly, the memorial program written for the funeral service noted: " . . . [she] made contributions of great significance to the Black Golf World for many years. She was a pioneer in both the Eastern Golf Association and the United Golfers Association."

Ethel Funches

Of the many fine black women golfers over the years, Ethel Funches probably came as close as anyone to matching the golfing exploits of Ann Gregory. Born in Owens, South Carolina, Funches moved to Washington, D. C. during the Depression years and got married in 1932. There were a number of similarities in the careers of Funches and Gregory. Both were born in the South and later migrated to northern cities; both were introduced to golf by their husbands; both started playing golf as adults; and both showed an immediate aptitude for the game. Captivated by golf in much the same way as her Indiana counterpart, Funches joined the Wake-Robin Golf Club in 1943.

At the end of her playing career, Funches had compiled a creditable amateur record. She won the UGA national women's championship an unprecedented five times, as well as a whole host of local and regional championships. Funches and Gregory played against each other on more than one occasion but there is no evidence that Funches ever succeeded in vanquishing her rival. Like Ann Gregory, Ethel Funches was often approached with offers to turn professional but she, too, refused. Their reasons for declining the offers, however, were different. Gregory believed that professional golf would interfere with family life. Funches, on the other hand, felt uneasy about playing in a predominantly white environment.(24) As a result, Funches restricted her golfing activities to the black circuit. In 1970, because of her golfing achievements in golf, the lively lady from northeast Washington, D. C. was inducted into the UGA Hall of Fame.

Althea Gibson

Ann Gregory's unmatched record became a source of inspiration to the next generation of black women golfers. Althea Gibson was one who sought to follow in Gregory's footsteps—but on the profes-

Althea Gibson, who won fame as an amateur tennis player, lines up a putt as she prepares for the 1965 USGA Women's Open.   (Credit: AP/World Wide Photo)

sional tour. Considering the fact that she had already been a trail-blazer and a major star in another sport, Gibson's goal was not too surprising.

She was born on August 25, 1927 in Silver, South Carolina. At the age of three, Althea was sent to live with an aunt in New York City. Growing up there, she took part in a variety of sports. In 1940, she was given her first tennis racket and began to take lessons from Fred Johnson at the Harlem River courts at 152nd Street and Seventh Avenue. One year later, she was good enough to compete in tournaments and promptly won her first event—the New York State Junior Girls. In 1945, she won her second straight national junior girls championship of the (all-black) American Tennis Association. Five years later, she became the first African American woman to compete in the national tournament of the United States Lawn Tennis Association (USLTA) at Forest Hills. As a singles player, she won her first Grand Slam event at the 1956 French Open. A year later, she won the women's singles championship at Wimbledon *and* the U.S. Open at Forest Hills. In 1958, she took both titles for the second time. By the end of the decade, Althea Gibson began to pursue other challenges.

In 1960, at the age of thirty-three, she began concentrating on golf. Within one year she was scoring in the eighties and had earned a reputation for her prodigious drives. In 1962 and 1963, Gibson won the Ray Mitchell North-South Women's Amateur Tournament in Miami, Florida. She turned professional in late 1963, and the following year became the first African American golfer on the LPGA circuit.

Gibson competed on the pro tour somewhat irregularly for a number of years. In 1970, she tied for first place in the Len Immke Buick Open but lost in a playoff. Plagued throughout her career by a lackluster short game and erratic putting, the former tennis champion withdrew from professional golf in the late 1970s.

Phyllis Meekins

In 1980, 20 years after she picked up a golf club for the first time, Phyllis Meekins became an LPGA-accredited golf instructor. Born in Orange, Virginia, in an era when golf was mostly a game for privileged white women, Meekins grew up without showing any interest in the game. During World War II, she enlisted in the Women's Army Corps and served overseas from 1942 to 1944. At the end of the war, she attended Virginia State College and, later, Drexel University in Philadelphia. During this period she played golf for the first time.

By 1969 she had won the UGA senior women's title and was playing competitively in the metropolitan Philadelphia area. A full-time government civil service worker and a full-time mom, Phyllis eventually became involved with junior golf. Upon retiring from her civil service position in 1973, Meekins began to concentrate on developing a junior golf instruction program. That year she established "PGM Clinics," her business entity, and started the instructional component in the basement of a local church. Since then, the program has expanded to provide junior golf camps each summer. One of her male graduates has become a PGA teaching professional, and other students have excelled in high school and college golf.

Now operating a newly-acquired golf education facility in northwest Philadelphia, Meekins, though proud of her achievements, realizes that much more needs to be done. Unwilling to be despondent about the future, she argues that "Children should have an alternative. We want them to learn about themselves." She firmly believes that "Golf can be a tool to develop the whole."(25)

Renee Powell

Renee Powell, the second black female to qualify for the LPGA Tour, began swinging a golf club at the age of three. Her "clubs" were a putter and a driver that her father had cut down for her use. In 1958, at the age of twelve, she entered her first tournament. During her adolescent years she won a number of UGA events. Attending Ohio State University, she became the first African American to captain the golf team of a major institution. In 1967, Powell joined the LPGA and played full-time for 12 years until she sustained an arm injury in 1979. After the 1972 season, she toured the Far East for the USO. In 1973, she won the LPGA Kelly Springfield Open in Queensland, Australia. Powell also lived in England for six years and conducted golf clinics and exhibitions in Africa for the U.S. Department of State.

For seven years she was the head professional at the Seneca Golf Course in Broadview Heights, Ohio. When her father retired as head professional at the family-owned Clearview Golf Course in Canton, Ohio, Renee resigned from Seneca to assume her father's position.

No stranger to racial insults during her earlier days in competitive golf, Powell now works diligently to not only stimulate minority golf interest but to establish a receptive atmosphere for young minority aspirants. She serves on the Girls' Junior Committee of the USGA and she promotes the annual Renee Powell Pro-Am Tournament raising funds for the U. S. Special Olympics. She sums up her philosophy by stating: "I've always tried to be a total person, not just a golfer. The beauty of golf goes far beyond playing the game."(26)

La Ree Pearl Sugg

When she made her debut in the 1995 Cup Noodles Hawaiian Ladies Open, La Ree Pearl Sugg was the first black golfer to appear on the LPGA Tour in 17 years. Born in 1970 in Petersburg, Virginia, La Ree was introduced to golf at the age of six by her maternal grandfather, Dr. James C. Nelson, a former educator and golf coach at Virginia State University. As her game developed, Sugg won over 30 junior golf titles between 1979 and 1988. At Matoaca High School in Ettrick, Virginia, she was captain of the boys' golf team. At UCLA, where she majored in English, La Ree was a member of the team that won the 1991 NCAA women's golf championship.

After graduating from college, the long-driving young woman spent three years on the European Tour with an indifferent record of success. In 1994, on her second attempt, she qualified for the LPGA Tour. She has struggled since then, and maintaining her competitive edge has proved to be a challenge to the Old Dominion native. However, she intends to persevere in achieving her goal of a top 125 ranking.(27)

―⚬――⚬―

Faced with the daunting twin challenges of being black and female, African American women golfers have repeatedly demonstrated a remarkable degree of resolve and patience. Despite having to overcome a number of obstacles, black women have earned their rightful place in golf history. Yet we know surprisingly little about these women. We need to know more about Rhoda Fowler, a 1962 UGA Hall of Fame inductee who, in 1955, had played in every important black golf tournament for the preceding 22 years. There is little written about Nathalie Price, who contributed a great deal to women's golf in the state of Rhode Island before suffering a tragic death. It should be learned who introduced the long-hitting, left-hander Eoline Thornton to former world heavyweight boxing champion Joe Louis and made him aware of her golfing potential. Will young Nikia Davis of New Orleans, Louisiana, obtain her card to play on the LPGA Tour? Does a hole-by-hole record exist of the 1954 match in which Julia Towns Siler defeated the formidable Patty Berg? The questions are seemingly endless.

And the answers are important.

8 | From the Clubhouse to the Courthouse

Often overlooked is the extent to which events in the golf world helped to influence legal opinions rendered during the struggle for civil rights. In truth, golf was a major legal battleground. The types of legal challenges brought by black golfers and their supporters—and the decisions that were handed down—provide an interesting perspective not only on the relatively straightforward matters relating to public accommodation, but also on the more complex issues concerning private property and the rights of an individual to associate with whomever he or she chooses. A review of black golf history would be incomplete without consideration of the battles that were waged in the nation's courts.

They may not have been the first to take their grievances before a court of law, but some of the black golfers in the Chicago area were among the earliest to gain press attention for their actions. If nothing else, they were persistent. In 1920—more than a quarter-century before the bus boycott in Montgomery, Alabama which many observers mark as the beginning of the civil rights era—Walter Speedy and a few of his golfing companions appeared in a Chicago courtroom to sue officials of the Jackson Park public golf course for refusing to allow them to play in a city Public Links tournament. Not one to retreat in the face of egregious racial injustice, Speedy had frequent encounters with police officials over the right to play on the public golf courses. On more than one occasion, he was arrested for his actions.(1)

Robert "Pat" Ball, another black Chicago golfer, and his playing companion, Elmer Stout, of Belleview, New Jersey, took legal action after being disqualified from playing in a 1928 national Public Links tournament in Philadelphia. Sponsored by the USGA, the tournament was in its third day before the pair was disqualified. With the help of legal counsel, the two men successfully obtained a temporary injunction that prevented the tournament from proceeding.(2) When USGA officials realized that the tournament could not resume, they reinstated Ball and Stout. Realizing that they were not welcome, but having proved their point, the two men withdrew.

In 1938, four black members of the Heart of America Golf Club in Kansas City, Missouri, filed a suit against the city's mayor and three members of the parks board for being refused the right to play on both of the Swope Park public golf courses. At the time, black golfers could only play on the nine-hole course; the eighteen-hole course was reserved for whites. The plaintiffs argued that the city's policy violated the United States Constitution, the Missouri Constitution, and the charter of Kansas City. They also charged " . . . that such action is a breach of the grant made by the late Colonel Thomas H. Swope, who had stipulated that there should be no segregation in the park."(3) The fact that nothing further appears in subsequent legal publications suggests that the case was dropped or settled out-of-court.

As World War II approached, the number of golf-related racial incidents increased. While not every incident resulted in a court challenge, it was evident that black golfers were resorting to legal remedies with increasing frequency. In 1939, the USGA rejected the applications of Louis Rafael Corbin and three other black golfers to play in the National Open. The four filed a formal protest but they were not allowed to play and the ultimate outcome of the protest was not reported. Later that same year, Alfred "Tup" Holmes was barred from the annual National Collegiate Athletic Association tournament. Again, the author could find no report on the final outcome.

Toward the latter part of 1940, Hubert Delany, Roy Wilkins, and Edward Morrow sued the Central Valley Golf Club in Orange

County, New York, for its refusal to allow the trio to play on the club's golf course.(4) At the time, Delany was New York City Tax Commissioner, Wilkins was assistant secretary of the NAACP (he later became its top official), and Morrow was assigned to the New York State Employment Service. After two years of legal wrangling, the case was lost on appeal.

Two months before Hitler's legions invaded Poland in September of 1939 to precipitate World War II, the black citizens of Washington, D. C. proudly attended the dedication of the Langston Golf Course built by the U. S. National Park Service. The nine-hole course—constructed after 15 years of petitioning, meetings, and letter writing—soon proved inadequate in meeting the golfing demands of the black community in the District of Columbia. Without any prospects for improvement in the situation, a small group of black golfers decided to take matters into their own hands and "invade" the public-but-segregated East Potomac Park Golf Course for a round of golf. Their decision precipitated one of the most widely publicized events in African American golf history.(5) In early July of 1941, a trio of black golfers, adhering to strategy that had been agreed upon earlier, was escorted by six U. S. Park Service police officers while the three played a round of golf at East Potomac Park. The Park Service had been forewarned and, fearing violence, had dispatched the officers to provide protection for the golfers. In addition to the six officers, the golfers were accompanied by Dr. George Adams, a respected Washington physician, and Edgar Brown, husband of Paris Brown, who was present in his capacity as director of the National Negro Council. Despite being greeted by rock-throwing and a chorus of catcalls and racial epithets, the men were able to complete their round because of the police presence. The hostile reception provoked an appeal by the black golfers to Secretary of the Interior Harold L. Ickes, under whose jurisdiction the federally-supported East Potomac Park course was operated. The golfers requested that the Secretary review the discriminatory policies that existed at the facility and remove the racial barriers. Ickes saw the legitimacy of their arguments and wrote: "They are taxpayers, they are citizens, and they have a right to play on public courses on the same basis as whites. To be sure, we have maintained a golf course for Negroes in Washington, but the cold fact is that we haven't kept it up and it is not surprising that Negroes do not care to play on it."(6)

But fierce resistance from the neighboring white community continued unabated. The next year, Wake-Robin Golf Club applied for a permit to use the East Potomac Park course as the site for its annual tournament. Permission was granted, but white opposition was so intense that Wake-Robin withdrew its request.

Pat Ball, like his friend and fellow Chicago golfer Walter Speedy, repeatedly found himself at the center of racial controversy. In 1942, he was involved in another brouhaha. By this time, Ball had been appointed the club professional at Palos Hills Golf Course (the first black golfer in Chicago to attain this status). Neither that distinction nor his credentials as a former UGA national professional champion, however, meant much to the officials of Chicago's exclusive Olympia Fields Country Club, the august Chicago District Golf Association, or the tradition-bound USGA—all of whom were principals in that year's Hale America tournament. When Ball, Clyde Martin (Joe Louis' golf instructor at the time), and five other capable black golfers applied to enter the tournament, their fees were accepted . . . then returned. An African American Chicago alderman, who was present when the incident occurred, threatened to take legal action.(7) The absence of any further mention in the legal publication *Illinois Digest: Table of Cases*, suggests that the matter was not pursued in the courts.

The number of legal challenges to discrimination in golf diminished during World War II, but reappeared with increased intensity when the war was over. There were a number of reasons for the renewed determination to explore legal redress. Some ex-servicemen (probably not very many) had played golf while on active duty without encountering racial difficulties, especially when stationed overseas; Jackie Robinson had broken the color barrier in major league baseball; golf was growing in popularity in the black community and neither the segregated public golf courses nor the few black-owned private courses were adequate to satisfy the burgeoning demand; and desegregation of the armed forces in 1948 not only added to the number of new black golfers, it also reinforced the belief—especially among former servicemen—that they were entitled to the unrestricted use of facilities supported by tax funds. Finally, there was a rising tide of expectations accompanying the return to peacetime. Among black youth, especially, there was a heightened level of militancy coupled with strident demands for an end to racial injustice. While pre-World War II legal challenges to racial discrimination in golf focused heavily on the rights of black amateurs, a dual strategy began to emerge *after* the war. In addition to continuing the struggle against public golf course discrimination, African American golfing activists began a concerted effort to end racial bias in the professional ranks.

Twenty-seven years after it was founded in 1916, the Professional Golfers Association of America inserted the infamous Section 1 of Article III into its constitution. This clause limited membership to "Professional Golfers of the Caucasian Race." Oddly enough (according to an article in *Golf World* dated August 3, 1990), the clause was a response to a request in 1943 "to include women as members." The article in *Golf World* also stated that the Michigan delegation proposed an amendment, eventually accepted, that resulted in the new clause. As noted earlier, when Dewey Brown was admitted into the organization in 1928, it was undoubtedly an oversight caused by the PGA's failure to recognize his true racial identity. After his expulsion from the organization in 1934, new applicants were scrutinized more carefully to prevent another "error." Officials were now more determined than ever to keep the membership lily white.

But denial of membership was an unending source of anger and humiliation for black professional golfers. Without that membership, black pros were prevented from competing for the high purses that were available on the PGA Tour. By the mid-1940s, there were only three predominantly white tournaments that allowed black professionals to enter—the Los Angeles Open, the Tam O' Shanter in Chicago, and the Canadian Open in Toronto. As a result, they were unable to maintain their skills at a high competitive level year-round. In addition, their status as "professionals" could be called into question because they were not afforded the opportunity to conform to the high standard of play that was set for white PGA members. The smoldering resentment increased with each passing day, and it was only a matter of time before the situation would erupt in a public confrontation. That momentous event occurred in 1948.

After playing in the Los Angeles Open the first week of the year,

both Ted Rhodes and William "Bill" Spiller were among the top finishers; Rhodes finished 21st and Spiller was 34th in a field of 66
players.(8) Tour rules at the time automatically qualified *all players*
who finished in the top 60 to play in the next scheduled Tour event.
That year, the Richmond Open, held near Oakland, California, was
next in line. Rhodes and Spiller paid their entry fees and traveled to
Oakland where they played two practice rounds. After the second
warm-up round, PGA tournament chairman George Schneiter approached Spiller and told him that he and Rhodes would not be allowed to continue because they were not PGA members. Infuriated
by the treatment they were receiving, Spiller stormed off and contacted Johnny Merrin, a college acquaintance living in nearby Berke-
ley, and told him what had happened. Merrin got in touch with Ira
Blue, an ABC sportscaster. Blue not only reported the ruling to his
radio audience, he lambasted the PGA for its decision as well.

The two golfers then met with Jonathan Rowell, an attorney who
had some experience combating racial discrimination in the San
Francisco area. Rowell agreed to represent Rhodes and Spiller without a fee. Together with Madison Gunther, a local black golfer who
had qualified to play in the Richmond Open but had also been
barred, Rhodes and Spiller filed suit against the PGA on January 17,
1948. The amount of the suit was $315,000, for denying them the
opportunity to obtain employment in their chosen profession. Each
of the golfers also sued Richmond Country Club, the venue of the
tournament, for $5000 in damages.

Three days after filing the suit, Rowell wrote to Thurgood Marshall who, at the time, was director-counsel of the NAACP Legal
Defense and Educational Fund based in New York City (later Marshall would be appointed an Associate Justice of the United States
Supreme Court). In his letter, Rowell made two interesting observa-
tions: "It is apparent," he wrote, "that the case filed on behalf of
these three men presents novel and important legal points." Believ-
ing that the litigation would be a lengthy process, he stated: "Likewise, it is highly probable that the case will be contested through
every possible court." Accordingly, even though he did not intend to
charge for his services, he felt that substantial expenses would be incurred in the preliminary phase of the proceedings and hoped that

". . . your organization could contribute this amount [$250] toward the payment of preliminary expenses."(9)

The outcome of Rowell's appeal to the NAACP is not known, but less than two months later Rowell met with the legal counsel representing the PGA and worked out an agreement in which the plaintiffs would drop the suit in return for a promise that the PGA would not discriminate against black golfers in the future. Rowell persuaded a highly skeptical Spiller to accept the arrangement and the suit was dropped. Instead of instigating the establishment of long-needed policies based on fair play, however, the agreement merely ushered in another era of PGA duplicity and hypocrisy.

Reacting to the negative publicity it received from its inept handling of the Richmond Open incident, the PGA resorted to a new ploy. PGA co-sponsored events were now referred to as "Open Invitationals." Besides being an oxymoronic contradiction in terms, the new name allowed a host club to refuse to "invite" a black golfer to an event, whereupon the PGA could wring its hands and declare it had no control over a private club's policies. With this new terminology in place, black golfers continued to be excluded from virtually every event on the all-white PGA Tour.

The next significant incident in this ongoing saga occurred in 1952, this time in San Diego, California. It involved heavyweight boxing champion Joe Louis, now a capable amateur golfer. The San Diego tournament that year was a charity event and Louis had been invited to play. Rhodes and Spiller were in the field as well. Shortly before the event began, however, all three were barred from participating. Louis' reaction to this was to contact columnist Walter Winchell, who broadcast the story on his popular radio program.

The result of Winchell's "news" was a barrage of telephone calls, telegrams, and letters sent to the PGA by listeners of his program. Reacting with astonishing speed, newly-elected PGA president Horton Smith convened a meeting in San Diego and invited Louis, Louis' confidante Leonard Reed, and a local black amateur golfer named Eural Clark. Either by accident or design, Spiller and Rhodes were not asked to attend. When he learned of his exclusion, the fiery Spiller, who happened to be in the same building where the meeting was taking place, strode into the room and confronted Smith in a testy exchange. Smith's attempts to soothe Spiller met with no suc-

Professional golfer Bill Spiller sat dejectedly at the first tee as golfers started their rounds in the 1952 San Diego Open Tournament. Spiller was ruled ineligible because of PGA rules.   (Credit: Bettmann Archives)

cess and Smith quickly realized that Spiller was not to be fooled with and was a formidable opponent. After a short, tense meeting, Spiller, who since 1948 had harbored grave doubts about the PGA's sincerity, left the room threatening to take legal action unless a way was found to satisfy the demands of black golfers.

Ex-heavyweight champion Joe Louis putts at the first green of the
1952 San Diego Open after initially being barred from the tournament.
(Credit: Bettmann Archives)

In the end, Joe Louis was permitted to play in the tournament but Rhodes and Spiller were not. Attempting to find a solution to the thorny problem facing the organization, Smith proposed a compromise that he allegedly discussed with Louis during a round they played together in San Diego. In his proposal, Smith suggested formation of a committee—composed of Louis, Spiller, Rhodes, Clark, and Howard Wheeler—that would select *one* black professional and *one* black amateur to play in each PGA co-sponsored event. This "Negro Golfing Committee" would act as a clearing house for the

PGA, but the latter would retain authority to make the final selection. The committee would also be charged with the responsibility of judging the "morals and manners" of candidates to be selected. When the black golfing community got wind of this outrageous nonsolution, it unleashed a firestorm of protest. Sportswriter Russ Cowans urged the individuals named to serve on the committee to ". . . disassociate themselves from it before the roof falls on them."(10) Faced with the groundswell of criticism, the proposal was dropped.

After the San Diego episode, the PGA amended its constitution to allow non-PGA members to play in tournaments *if* they received an invitation from a sponsor. Designated as "approved entries," the new status enabled Rhodes and Spiller to play in many tournaments from which they would have been barred previously. Still, those in the "approved entry" class did not have any voting rights in the PGA and they remained at the mercy of sponsors to receive invitations. Most importantly, they were not full-fledged members of the PGA.

Shortly after the incident in southern California, Smith wrote an article in *Golf Life* that offered a facile, if convoluted, explanation and defense of the recent actions taken by the PGA. After providing a brief summary of his activities leading up to the event, Smith wrote:

> Then came San Diego as a new sponsor on the Schedule. . . . Here we were hit smack in the face with the Negro question. This is a very difficult problem because the Negro question is bigger than golf, being not only national in scope but international as well.
>
> Here, I would like to say that I believe it has been demonstrated that golfers are excellent sports and fairminded individuals. Also that the P. G. A. has a great responsibility in choosing its players. In this respect the P. G. A. has to assume much control to supervise and discipline its players, especially if it is to help in the expansion and promotion of golf.(11)

Smith emphasized further that "P. G. A. members are actually guests at the host club in a P. G. A. co-sponsored tournament and our tournaments are not a public open tournament for the above mentioned reasons." Pleased with what he believed were progressive accomplishments of his organization, Smith proudly continued. "So, therefore, the P. G. A. eliminated any discriminating clauses in its tournament rules." Studiously avoided was any reference to the "Caucasian Race" clause which remained in the PGA constitution. Perhaps the most glaring falsehood appeared in Smith's concluding paragraph. "As a footnote," he wrote, "I would like to add that seemingly the Phoenix and Tucson tournaments [which followed the San Diego Open] went forward without incident."

Indeed, after San Diego, Bill Spiller, Ted Rhodes, and Charlie Sifford, together with amateurs Joe Louis, Leonard Reed, Eural Clark and Joe Roach, did go to Arizona to attempt to qualify for the Phoenix Open. After being denied use of the locker-room facilities, Louis, Rhodes, Sifford, and Clark were sent out as the first group of the morning in the qualifying round. At the first green, they were greeted by the revolting sight and smell of human excrement that someone had surreptitiously placed in the cup.(12) So much for "excellent sports and fairminded individuals."

Not surprisingly, Bill Spiller played an important part in the final chapter of the African American struggle to obtain unrestricted PGA membership. In early January of 1960, now past his prime and in dire financial straits, Spiller was compelled to return to caddying to make ends meet. One morning at the Hillcrest Country Club in Los Angeles, Spiller was assigned to caddie for club member Harry Braverman. As they walked together over the course, Braverman heard the story of Spiller's career and the difficulties that he had encountered while trying to earn a living as a touring golf professional. Braverman's response was to ask Spiller to provide him with written information. In a letter to Braverman dated January 6, 1960, Spiller briefly listed the situations he had faced since 1948.(13) Braverman sent the letter to California Attorney General Stanley Mosk. On the basis of Spiller's letter and additional information he had gathered, Mosk informed the PGA that if it continued to discriminate against black golfers, it would not be allowed to hold tournaments on any of the public golf courses in California. In its reply, the PGA stated that henceforth it would use only *private* courses for its events.

Fearlessly, Mosk countered by telling the PGA that it would not be allowed to circumvent his ruling by using private courses. Moreover,

The Honorable Stanley Mosk.
(Credit: Stanley Mosk)

Mosk notified the attorneys general in other states of the action he had taken. Faced with the realization that Mosk was not bluffing and was resolute in his determination to implement the ruling, the PGA capitulated. In November 1961, the offensive and disgraceful "Caucasian Race" clause was deleted from the PGA constitution. A shameful chapter in American golf history had finally come to an end.

—⫘⫘—

On several occasions after the "Caucasian only" clause was inserted into the constitution of the PGA in 1943, a number of state sections—

Michigan and Southern California among them—attempted to have it removed. Each effort to bring the proposal to a vote, however, was blocked by disagreeing sections—many of them from the South. Ironically perhaps (according to the previously-mentioned 1990 article in Golf World), when the clause was finally eliminated in 1961 the amendment to do so was co-sponsored by the Georgia-Alabama delegation.

—⁓——⁓—

William "Bill" Spiller

One of the major figures in African American golf history, William "Bill" Spiller was so much a part of the struggle to eliminate racial barriers to PGA membership that a false image of the man might emerge if his life were viewed as separate and distinct from that struggle. For more than four decades, the battle he waged against racism in the corridors of professional golf consumed his very being. It affected his personality, his ability to earn a living, and ultimately his health. This brief portrait is not a sequel to the earlier section on the PGA, it is an integral part of the evolutionary continuum of someone who has not been accorded the recognition he deserves.

Perhaps the angriest of a generation of angry black professional golfers when he went to his grave in 1988 at the age of 75, Bill Spiller was ill-tempered, embittered , and forsaken by all but his closest relatives and a few loyal friends. Because he felt so strongly that he'd been wronged, and singled-out for speaking his mind, much of his adult life was punctuated by hurt and, as the end neared, his brooding rage sometimes pushed him to the brink of violence.

In his book *Gettin' To The Dance Floor*, golf writer Al Barkow provides one of the most complete accounts of Spiller's life. The diminutive Spiller was born in 1913 in the county seat of Tishimingo, Oklahoma, located in the south central section of the state. At the age of nine, he went to live with his father in Tulsa and there he completed elementary and high schools. He then attended Wiley College, an all-black institution in Marshall, Texas, where he majored in sociology and education. After graduation, the best job he could find paid only $60 a month. Unwilling to work for a pittance, he moved to Los Angeles in 1938 to live with his mother while seeking employment. After eight disappointing months, he accepted a job as a redcap in the newly-opened Los Angeles railroad station.

Bill Spiller did not start playing golf until 1942 at the age of twenty-nine, but within four years he had won most of the black golf tournaments in southern California. Just about that time he met Ted Rhodes who, through Joe Louis' largesse, was receiving instruction from teaching professional Ray Mangrum. Spiller frequently accompanied Rhodes to his lessons and would watch from the sidelines to pick up tips that might improve his own game. To gain experience playing on the better golf courses, he took a waiter's job for four months at the Los Angeles Country Club where caddies and other service help could play at designated times. Constantly struggling to support himself and his family, Spiller also worked for the post office and a doughnut shop. Once, after an all-day match, Spiller won enough money from Joe Louis to buy a modest home.(14)

In one of his interviews with Barkow, Spiller stated: "I hated prejudice with a passion." From early childhood he deeply resented racial insults—real or imagined. One of the few black professional golfers of his generation with a college degree, Spiller was unwilling to behave deferentially in the presence of whites, especially those whose level of educational attainment obviously was less than his. With his flinty personality, short fuse, and strong aversion to racial injustice, he was constantly involved in one racially-tinged episode after another. He got into an ugly staring match with dancer/movie star Fred Astaire when the entertainer snubbed him during a qualifying round played at the Bel Air Country Club in Los Angeles. Another time, he challenged PGA president Horton Smith to a fist fight over an alleged remark made by Smith. After he and four other black golfers were prevented from participating in the 1952 San Diego Open, Spiller stood on the first tee refusing to allow the tournament to begin.

By 1953, the Oklahoma-born golfer was back on the black golf circuit. Over the next few years he won a number of these events, but the sporadic prize money was insufficient to support himself and his family. Seeking steady employment, Spiller applied for positions as assistant professional or teaching professional at six public courses in the Los Angeles area. He also passed a civil service examination for the position of golf starter in the city of Los Angeles. In each instance, he failed to get the job. Now a dejected man, he often expressed his frustrations to columnist-activist Maggie Hathaway. To be forced by circumstances to return to caddying in 1960 was the final insult and the most difficult for him to accept.

In the opinion of some, Bill Spiller was a "hot-head." Others were inclined to label him as a "racist in reverse." True, there were times when he was impatient with the stifling status quo. A proud man, he refused to accept the notion of staying in his "place." He felt he was entitled to fair treatment and he steadfastly refused to settle for less. Following his mother's precepts, he did not hate white people. A few of his white fellow professionals were friends, and he had kind words for Jimmy Demaret, Lawson Little, and Sam Snead.(15) Bill Spiller paid a high price for his convictions, but golf is the beneficiary of his resolve. Two years before his death in 1988, he was inducted into the UGA Golf Hall of Fame.

The PGA never acted on the membership application that he filed in 1948.

Without a meticulous search of court records at the lowest judicial level, it is impossible to determine the true magnitude of the trials and tribulations endured by the postwar generation of black golfers in their quest for unrestricted access to public golf facilities. Relying solely on items published in black newspapers, the NAACP files on deposit in the Library of Congress, and cases published in the *Race Relations Law Reporter*, 33 cases were identified by the author in which black golfers resorted to legal action between 1945 and 1966. From all indications, this figure is a fraction of the true number. It is likely that accurate data would reveal that the actual numbers are much higher.

If for no other reason than the small number, any analysis of the 33 cases is open to question. Besides, certain important details of each case are unknown. These include the chronology of events, number of plaintiffs, costs incurred, and the identity of civil rights organizations (if any) that were involved in the litigation. Despite these limitations, a review of the cited cases offer a few valuable insights.

Firstly, a variety of strategies were employed by defendants to circumvent the charges brought against them. Some public courses were sold or leased to private owners. New "separate but equal" golf courses were built or promised. In one of the most widely publicized cases, six black golfers were arrested and jailed for 30 days for trespassing on a golf course in Greensboro, North Carolina.

Secondly, no section of the country was immune to public golf course discrimination. Of the 33 cases, eight (nearly one-quarter) occurred outside the southern United States. In the end, of course, black golfers prevailed.

With the passage of civil rights legislation in the mid- and late-1960s, racial discrimination in the use of *public* golf facilities effectively came to an end. As far as access to *private* facilities was concerned, the situation remained more or less the same until a modicum of change occurred in 1990. In the spring of that year, Hall Thompson, president of the Shoal Creek Country Club in Birmingham, Alabama, told a local newspaper that African Americans would not be accepted to membership in the club. His ill-chosen, racist remarks caused serious repercussions. Shoal Creek was to be the site of the annual PGA Championship later that August. Fearing negative publicity upon hearing of the club's exclusionary policy, a number of major corporations withdrew their commercials from the televised broadcasts. This cost the network millions of dollars in lost advertising revenue. Following the infamous event, the PGA and PGA Tour announced that it would no longer use private clubs as tournament sites if the clubs had any kind of a discriminatory membership policy. The United States Golf Association, in turn, reiterated its long-standing decision that no USGA event would be held at any golf course—private or public—that practiced racial discrimination. Consequently, the few clubs that believed they had the right to select their members as they saw fit, either dropped out as current sites or withdrew their invitations to become future sites.

Other clubs, however, recoiling from the adverse Shoal Creek publicity and the possibility of lost income from PGA, PGA Tour, and/or USGA tournaments, began to scramble for "acceptable" black recruits. In the ensuing years, a number of clubs opened their doors to one or two black members. Although this is a slight improvement over what existed formerly, it is too early to view these developments as a cause for jubilation. In the cold light of reality, little of substance has changed, and there are few indications that private country clubs will become oases of multiculturalism in the foreseeable future.

Gaining membership in private (white) country clubs is a complex issue for black golfers. At first glance, because exclusionary policies are inherently unjust, it may seem only fitting and proper to contest them wherever and whenever possible. Some African Americans, especially those in corporate executive positions, argue that being unable to secure private club membership denies them the opportunity to make important business contacts and solidify valuable business negotiations. Moreover, they assert that lacking private club membership, their children are unable to make contacts that may prove helpful in later life.(16) These statements undeniably are true. But there are other issues lurking beneath the surface that raise (or should raise) troubling concerns. If the day ever comes when African Americans obtain unrestricted access to membership in private country clubs, they will face an ethical dilemma: it will then be their task to help explain what criteria (other than wealth) should be used to determine membership eligibility. The shoe will be on the other foot, as they say, and it will be interesting to see how African Americans deal with this situation.

Within the realm of private property considerations is the bedeviling possibility that the taxes paid by private country clubs may not cover the total costs (direct and indirect) for goods and services that are provided to the clubs from the public coffers. This is a matter of particular concern in instances where a private club receives tax abatements from a local municipality. This has led one observer to point out that " . . . many individuals concede the right of private clubs to select their membership and to exclude whomever [it chooses]. However, such clubs should not at the same time receive public benefits. [It amounts to a situation where] tax-paying citizens actually subsidize the clubs."(17) If careful cost analyses substantiate these claims, it then raises important legal questions about the "private" designation under which these clubs function.

In a somewhat curious but related statement made in May of 1997, President Bill Clinton remarked that "people of all ages and walks of life should have the opportunity to compete on the best courses our country has to offer."(18) It would be interesting to learn how this laudable goal might be achieved without abridging the rights of private property and freedom of association—fundamental principles underlying the social order.

A full discussion of the complex legal, political, moral, and socioeconomic issues involved in an equitable resolution of country club membership lies well outside the scope of this book. Suffice it to say that African Americans will continue to play a larger part in the ongoing debate.

9 | Benefactors, Boosters, and Businessmen

During the course of their long involvement with the game of the Scots, black golfers have been fortunate to have people who were willing to be of assistance. The forms of assistance were as varied as the personalities of those providing it. Sometimes, help was provided through financial gifts or loans. Sometimes it came in the form of emotional support, marital counseling, and moral guidance. Sometimes it was simply an article in a newspaper. Generally, it was a solitary person who provided help (there are no examples of individuals combining resources to develop a broader base of support). Because of what they did, this section is a tribute to those men and women, black and white, who used their talents or personal resources for the betterment of black golf. Without their efforts, the road would have been rockier and the journey longer.

Unheralded Black Scribes

At a two-day sports symposium in December of 1996, Reverend Jesse Jackson called attention to the minuscule number of African American sports columnists working for the mainstream press. Directing his displeasure at the white media, Reverend Jackson noted that only 10 of the nation's 1,600 daily newspapers employed a black columnist.(1) Of that small number, it was unlikely that any of them restricted their coverage solely to golf. Even today, there is only the occasional mention of predominantly black golf events in the major daily newspapers, and little attention is given to issues that affect black golfers. The situation, of course, was much worse during the earlier years of this century. Although a relatively small fraction of the total playing population, black golfers—then and now—have been interested in learning about events taking place in their cloistered golf world. Over time, black sports columnists on the staffs of black newspapers played an important role in bringing this information to the attention of African American golfers, and it was to these newspapers that the black golfing community turned.

Even though their readership was small in comparison to black newspapers in the large urban centers of Chicago, Detroit, Pittsburgh, Washington D.C., New York, and Philadelphia, there were publications in some of the smaller cities where black sportswriters were eager to report on activities on the links. These writers had to cover a variety of sporting events in addition to golf and, as might be expected, the focus of their golf articles was on local events. Joel W. Smith published his column "Down the Fairway" in the *Atlanta Daily World*, and Oliver Terry wrote "Teeing' Off" for the *California Eagle*. The importance of these somewhat obscure columns was that they were written as early as 1941, antedating golf columns in better-known black newspapers by nearly a decade. Unfortunately, information about the subsequent careers of both men is unavailable.

For much of the twentieth century, most of the information about black golf history centers around the activities of golfers in two sections of the country east of the Mississippi River. Chicago, and to a lesser extent Detroit, were the focal points in the Midwest. In the eastern part of the country, African American golf events were reported with frequency from Pittsburgh, Philadelphia, the District of Columbia, and the metropolitan areas of New York City. An important reason why this occurred was the existence of influential black newspapers in and around these densely populated urban centers. In the Midwest, it was the *Chicago Defender* and the *Michigan Chronicle* (based in Detroit). On the East Coast, the *Pittsburgh Courier*, the *New York Amsterdam News* and the Baltimore-based *Afro-American* were the influential black newspapers. In 1927, four of these publications (the *Michigan Chronicle* did not exist at the time) were rated by one observer as the "best all-around newspapers."(2) The combined readership was substantial, and many of the readers were avid sports fans. To satisfy reader demand, each of the prominent black newspapers had strong sports sections in which golf received a fair amount of attention.

Yet somewhat paradoxically, the individual who probably was the nation's first African American golf reporter was neither a resident of the previously mentioned focal centers nor did he serve as a golf reporter for the black press. Lester A. Walton was born in St. Louis, Missouri on April 20, 1882. At the age of twenty, he began working as a reporter for the white *St. Louis Star Sayings* (which later became the *St. Louis Star-Times*) and then was hired by the *St. Louis Globe-Democrat*. Shocked when he discovered that Walton was black, the city editor of the *Globe-Democrat* decided, nevertheless, to retain the fledgling reporter on the staff. Over the course of a variety of assignments on the newspaper, Walton became a competent golf reporter.(3)

In 1908, Walton moved to New York City and was drama editor for the black-owned *New York Age* for six years. During this period he also served as manager of the Lafayette Theater, a landmark theatrical playhouse in Harlem. He returned to journalism in 1922 when he became a staff columnist for the white *New York World*. While there he wrote a series of feature articles, one of which dealt with the Shady Rest Golf & Country Club. Over his varied and distinguished career, Lester A. Walton served on the Democratic National Committee, was a newspaper correspondent at the post-World War I Versailles Peace Conference, was appointed U.S. envoy extraordinary and minister plenipotentiary to Liberia from 1935 to 1936, and was elected to be the advisor to the Liberian delegation to the United Nations from 1946 to 1949. Walton died in New York City on October 16, 1965.

Despite the slow but steady increase in golf's popularity among blacks during the first half of the twentieth century, a major preoccupation among black sportswriters during most of these years was the exclusion of African Americans from organized baseball. Led by the energetic Wendell Smith, sportswriter for the *Pittsburgh Courier*, a concerted 12-year crusade was mounted to lift the ban.(4) Jackie Robinson's 1947 breakthrough into baseball enabled black sportswriters to turn their attention to other areas of athletic competition. One of those writers was Russell J. Cowans.

Called "Russ" by almost everyone who knew him, Cowans was born in Chicago in 1899. After completing elementary school, he moved on to Wendell Phillips High School. In 1935, he went to Detroit as Joe Louis' first personal secretary, a position he held until 1937, when Louis became the world's heavyweight boxing champion. During this time he also covered the city beat as a reporter for the Detroit edition of the *Chicago Defender*.

Following his employment by Louis, Cowans joined the staff of the *Michigan Chronicle* where, in addition to continuing his coverage of Detroit local affairs, he began to develop an interest in black professional baseball. When black sportswriters formed their own organization in 1940, he was elected secretary. In 1945, Russ married Thelma Simmons McTyre, a notable black golfer. The next year, he became the first black reporter to travel the black golf circuit on a more or less regular basis. This enabled him to cover golf from coast and to coast and solicit ideas for his column from golfers across the country.(5) In 1948, he covered the Olympic Games in London, and in 1949 became the sports editor of the *Chicago Defender*, succeeding the renowned veteran Frank A. "Fay" Young.

A golfer himself, one of Cowans' greatest satisfactions was his weekly golf column published in the *Defender* during the summer months. Started in 1950, it was the first golf column to appear with regularity in any of the large black newspapers and it was published in a newspaper which claimed to be the black weekly that consistently reported more news about golf than any of the others. In his "Down the Fairway" column, Cowans (who often used the pseudonym "Tee Shot") stated that he intended it " . . . to be devoted to the activities of the average golfers—those boys and gals who never grab the headlines by winning a major tournament."(6) Over the nine years that the column appeared, "Tee Shot" stuck to his promise. Invariably filled with a wide assortment of local golf news, the columns also carried items of interest that occurred at Rivervale Country Club in Bergen County, New Jersey; Lake Chabot Golf Course in Oakland California; New Lincoln Country Club in Atlanta, Georgia; and Swope Park Number One Course in Kansas City, Missouri. The stories were usually written in a breezy, informal style.

One of the last "Down the Fairway" columns—a short instructional piece on putting—appeared in July of 1959. Perhaps "Tee Shot" was now so involved with administrative and other journalistic activities that he was unable to continue his golf coverage.

It was difficult to determine exactly when Cowans became ill, but an obituary published at the time of his death on December 27, 1978, mentioned that he succumbed after a lengthy illness. Known for his jaunty attire, the short, wiry man—who at one time served as president of the Windy City Golf Club—was highly respected by his colleagues and a wide circle of friends and associates in the black golf community. He left a praiseworthy legacy of golf reporting for the generations that would follow.

In 1958, some eight years after Russ Cowans started his weekly golf columns, Franklin T. Lett, Sr. became the golf editor of the *Michigan Chronicle*. Born in Battle Creek, Michigan, Lett was a three-time All-State basketball player at Battle Creek High School. His first brush with racial discrimination occurred when he graduated from high school and was barred from playing on the basketball team at the University of Michigan. From that moment on, Lett turned his attention to golf.(7)

During his lifetime, he devoted much of his considerable energy to the promotion of junior golf and to waging a tireless battle against the exclusion of qualified black golfers from the Masters Tournament. A firm believer in the need for strong black organizations to advance black golfing objectives, Lett served six terms as president of the Detroit Amateur Golf Club, six terms as president of the Midwest district chapter of the UGA, and six years as president of the UGA. He was also one of the travel consultants for International Golf Tours, the New York City-based travel agency. In 1962, he was inducted into the UGA Hall of Fame.

Lett's columns in the *Chronicle* tended to focus on a single issue or personality. When he wrote about more than a single subject, it usually concerned local golf events. Although he traveled widely in the United States and made several golf trips abroad, he seldom mentioned his personal golf activities. When he died in May of 1973, Franklin T. Lett, Sr. left an indelible imprint—both literally and figuratively—on African American golf history.

Veteran sportswriter Samuel H. Lacy, Sr. was born in Mystic, Con-

necticut in 1903. His mother was a Shinnecock Indian and his father
was an African American. Two years after his birth, his family moved
to Washington D.C. where he went to elementary school and high
school. As an adolescent, he caddied for a short time at Columbia
Country Club in Maryland. After one year at Howard University in
his hometown, Lacy left to pursue a career in semiprofessional baseball. Unfortunately, his days on the diamond were cut short by a
wrist injury so he returned to Howard and graduated in 1932.
Shortly after getting his degree, he became sports editor of the
Washington Tribune where he remained until 1940 when he left to
join the staff of the *Chicago Defender*. After three years in Chicago,
he returned to Washington D.C. There he joined the staff of the
Afro-American newspaper and started "A to Z", the column for
which he is best known.

Lacy's columns, though wide-ranging, focused heavily on baseball, boxing, and football. Like his colleague Frankin Lett, Lacy usually focused on a single issue when he wrote about golf. In 1965, he
congratulated the Columbia Broadcasting System for including black
golfers in its "CBS Golf Classic" television program.(8) When he
was excluded from a golf tournament in 1972, he wrote a satirical
but withering denunciation of racial discrimination in the golf world.
In 1974, he chided Johnny Miller, Arnold Palmer, and Jack Nicklaus
for opposing the ruling by the commissioner of the PGA's Tournament Players Division that required top golfers to play in three designated events. A recipient of numerous awards and an honorary degree from Morgan State University (in 1995), Samuel H.Lacy, Sr. is
a venerated figure in sports journalism. He is someone who loves
golf and is prepared to do battle against those who demean the game
with bigotry, greed, or snobbishness.

Any narrative concerning earlier African American golf writers
would be incomplete without an account of the life and times of the
doughty Maggie Hathaway. Born in Shreveport, Louisiana, sometime in the early 1920s (she alleges that her family did not keep birth
certificates!), Maggie was one of seven children.(9) She received her
early education in Shreveport where she played on the high school
girl's basketball team for four years.

After arriving in Los Angeles in 1954, she worked for a while in
the film industry during which—among other things—she served as

a double for the famed singer/entertainer Lena Horne. She later obtained employment as a community worker in the Head Start program. In 1955, Maggie began playing golf after wagering with former heavyweight boxing champion Joe Louis that she could hit a golf ball on her first attempt. She won and has continued to play whenever the opportunity presents itself. Not long after she began playing, she discovered that black golfers in the Los Angeles area were excluded from many public and private courses. This led her, in 1958, to start a campaign to gain membership in the all-white Western Avenue Women's County Golf Club. After four years, during which she was compelled to sue the Women's Public Links Association, black golfers were admitted—all except Maggie, who was placed on a waiting list. Finally, in 1970, she was awarded honorary membership.

In 1962, Hathaway organized the Beverly Hills chapter of the National Association for the Advancement of Colored People (NAACP), and the following year she was instrumental in starting the well-known NAACP Image Awards for outstanding black achievers. Not one to rest on her laurels, she also formed Minority Associated Golfers, an organization that exerted pressure for African Americans to be employed at pro shops and to participate in the full range of activities at celebrity golf tournaments.(10)

Hathaway's career in journalism also started in 1962 when she began writing a column for the *California Eagle*. In 1963, the paper was sold and she moved to the *Los Angeles Sentinel* where she remained until her retirement in 1996. In addition to her weekly golf columns, she wrote occasional feature stories. Her golf columns covered the landscape. She provided information on large and small golf events; criticized Gary Player at a Pebble Beach event during the apartheid era in South Africa; promoted NAACP activities; introduced young golfers (particularly black females) to the public; castigated the LPGA; and took blacks to task for being unwilling to shoulder important responsibilities. When proved wrong, such as the time she criticized Bing Crosby for failing to invite black golfers to the tournament named after him, she apologized in her column for all to read. Her column no longer appears, but Maggie Hathaway remains a cherished figure in the golf community, especially on the West Coast.

A few other black sportswriters commented on golf matters from time to time, but they were less well-known. Included among them are John Glover, who succeeded Franklin Lett at the *Michigan Chronicle*, and Edward Hargrove of the *Afro-American*. Frank Saunders, sports editor of the *Michigan Chronicle*, was a dedicated golfer and an active supporter of the Michigan Chronicle Golf League. Though neither a sportswriter nor a golf writer *per se*, Dan Burley, the colorful editor and satirist, penned occasional items pertaining to golf in the *New York Amsterdam News*.

Each of the black golf writers tried to provide their respective readerships with a wide range of relevant information, yet each had a particular slant or theme. Russ Cowans lived up to his pledge to report on the run-of-the-mill black golfer; Maggie Hathaway stressed material pertaining to black women golfers; and both Franklin Lett and John Golver, especially the latter, used their columns to promote junior golf. Glover repeatedly deplored the small number of young blacks playing the game and was outspokenly critical of the lethargy displayed by black golfers regarding the situation. He once wrote: "The black golfing community has an obligation to expose our youth to golf simply because a void exists. There just aren't many black youth playing the game and very few winners among those who are playing."(11)

Joseph Louis Barrow

It was as if he sensed that in the not-too-distant future, golf would enjoy an explosive burst of popularity in the black community. He was on the scene when it happened, and his presence had a significant impact on what might be considered "the golden years" of black golf.

In 1936, the year before he was crowned world heavyweight boxing champion, the "Brown Bomber" began playing golf. According to one account, he was introduced to the game by sportswriters Hype Igoe and Walter Stewart. Another version credits journalist/impresario Ed Sullivan with getting him started. Although the identity of the individuals(s) who first enticed him into taking up the game is uncertain, Louis himself was quoted as stating unequivocally that the year was 1936.(1)

Within three years after he started playing, under the watchful eye of his Bermuda-born teaching professional Louis Rafael Corbin, Joe Louis was shooting in the low eighties. He became completely addicted to the game and his managers had to keep a tight rein on him lest he sacrifice his training in the ring for the pleasure of the fairways. One of his managers, John W. Roxborough, restricted Louis' golfing to every other day while he was training for a bout. "If we let Joe have his way," Roxborough declared, "he would play golf every day in addition to his road work. This would be entirely too much exercise and there would be the danger of his going stale."(2)

With each passing year, Louis became increasingly active in black golf events. He started by playing in a few local matches, and before long he was participating in larger black tournaments. Because of his enormous popularity, his presence on a golf course attracted large galleries. In 1940, when he played in the Eastern Golf Association Championships at Langston Golf Course in Washington, D. C., it was estimated that some 2,000 people were on hand each day of the three-day event—primarily to catch a glimpse of the Brown Bomber. Around this same time, Louis began taking a greater interest in promoting black golf. In August of 1941, six weeks after his successful title defense against Billy Conn, he sponsored the Joe Louis Open at Detroit's Rackham Golf Course. Louis played in the event *and* put up the entire $1,000 prize purse. One indication of the recognition he received for his activities in fostering golf among African Americans can be gleaned from a 1941 article in the *Atlanta Daily World*. "To further lend his moral support to place Negro golf in the upper bracket of public interest," the article stated, "Louis is also competing in the annual United Golfers Association national tournament in Boston. Only a fortnight ago, Joe participated in the Eastern Open in Pittsburgh."(3)

Under additional instruction from Clyde Martin, a young teaching professional from Washington, D. C., Louis' golf skills continued to improve. By the time he was inducted into the Army in 1942, he was scoring consistently in the mid-seventies. In the Army, Louis was initially assigned to a cavalry detachment at Fort Riley, Kansas. Whenever the opportunity presented itself, Louis played golf. Later,

Joe Louis tries out a new putter by his protégé Bill Spiller at the 1952 Phoenix Open.
Spiller was allowed to play after a change in the PGA's "Non-Caucasian" ruling.
(Credit: Bettmann Archives)

when he was sent to England to entertain U. S. troops, he spent his spare time playing golf in cities such as Liverpool and Manchester.

Within months after the end of the war in Europe, the second Joe Louis Open was held in July of 1945, once again at Rackham in Detroit. Though still in the army, Louis received special permission from his superiors to participate in the event. In 1946, Louis increased the tournament's purse to $2,000 and women were invited to compete for the first time. Because he was so popular, and a good golfer as well, he played frequently with celebrities such as Clark Gable, Bing Crosby, Fred Astaire, and Bob Hope, and with notable professionals Ben Hogan, Jimmy Demaret, Lawson Little, and Byron Nelson.

In almost every one of his published interviews, Louis talked about his golf game. It was apparent to many that he was growing increasingly disinterested in boxing, but it was equally apparent that he needed the income from boxing to support his lavish lifestyle. In the summer of 1948, he announced that "I'm hanging up my gloves after the fight with (Joe) Walcott and then I can play all the golf I want."(4) To some observers, Louis gave the distinct impression that boxing was interfering with his golfing aspirations. He was particularly disappointed and frustrated that he never won any of the five tournaments that he sponsored.

After the Brown Bomber finally retired from the ring in 1949, he lived up to his promise to concentrate on golf. Over the next two years there were newspaper accounts of him playing in Cleveland, Detroit, Atlanta, and Montreal. Being a well-known sports figure, he also received many invitations to play at white country clubs across the U.S. In spite of these opportunities, he was well aware that top black golfers were not being invited to the major tournaments. In one reference to Ted Rhodes, Charlie Sifford, and Bill Spiller, Louis commented: "God, those guys were great. If they had been white, or at least allowed to play in white tournaments, no telling where they'd have gone. They'd have had the big money and the time to develop themselves even more."(5)

Louis continued to chafe at the double standard, but seemingly did little about it until 1950. That year, he wrote to his friend Bing Crosby and complained about the treatment black golfers were receiving at the California tournament that was named after the entertainer. Not known for making public pronouncements about racial discrimination, Louis reached the end of his tether at the 1952 San Diego Open. There, with the help of columnist Walter Winchell, Louis exposed the hypocrisy of the PGA. He then went to the tournaments in Tucson and Phoenix to help in the process of chipping away at (but not totally eliminating) the PGA's exclusionary policies.

Joe Louis' reputation for gambling was well known, even though some of the stories have probably been exaggerated. Many a golfer, nevertheless, benefited from wagers against Louis, especially during his early playing days. As sportswriter Russ Cowans observed: "Joe has proven [to be] the financial angel of Negro golf."(6)

Louis remained an avid golfer until his health began to deteriorate in the late 1960s. Beset with financial and domestic problems, Louis suffered a series of emotional crises that precipitated mental deterioration. He played an occasional round of golf but had become a shadow of his former self. Unfortunately, both on and off the course, the Brown Bomber became a sad figure. When he died on April 12, 1981, his enormous contributions to boxing were recalled but there was scant mention that the world of golf —especially the world of black golf—had lost a major supporter.

For his contributions to the black golfing community, Joseph Louis Barrow was inducted into the UGA Hall of Fame in 1972. In 1986, a new Chicago golf course was named in his honor.

Jackie Robinson

While the phlegmatic Joe Louis seldom publicly confronted racially prejudiced golf officials or professionals, the opposite was true for Jackie Robinson. Like Bill Spiller, the petulant baseball star was eager to take on anyone who was racially biased. Robinson held strong views on many subjects, some of which were beyond his expertise.(7) He had, however, earned his stripes battling racial discrimination in major league baseball. Consequently, he felt he was justified to express his views on the subject. In 1956, after he retired from baseball, a column under his byline was published in the *New York Post*. While somewhat presumptuous, Robinson took on the role of civil rights spokesman. The column, which appeared two or three times a week, provided him with an excellent forum. A number of these columns, in whole or in part, were devoted to racial discrimination in golf.

An outstanding athlete prior to deciding on professional baseball, Robinson attended the University of California at Los Angeles (UCLA). While there—in addition to playing varsity baseball, football, and basketball—he played golf and tennis and swam. During

World War II, Robinson entered the Army. For a brief period, he and Joe Louis were stationed together at Fort Riley, Kansas, and the two played golf together a number of times.(8) While perhaps not as totally consumed by golf as Louis, Robinson enjoyed the game immensely and had an abiding interest in providing opportunities for black golfers.

In one of his early newspaper columns, Robinson expressed annoyance with the producers of a television golf series for their unwillingness to invite Charlie Sifford to compete in one of the matches. Knowing of Sifford's golfing competence, Robinson wrote: "It seems to me that the sponsors of these programs have nothing to lose and possibly a lot to gain by recognizing Sifford."

The following week, Robinson announced that he planned to attend the Baseball Players' Golf Tournament in Miami as he had for the previous five or six years. He was pleased that there were no racial restrictions, a contrast to what he had observed at many northern golf courses. He also expressed the hope that more cities would follow Miami's example and open their doors for all golfers to participate so that the nation could become "a truly democratic society."(9)

A month later, thoroughly incensed by what he saw happening in the sport, Robinson devoted an entire column to a scathing denunciation of racial discrimination in mainstream golf. "Golf," he wrote, "is the one major sport in America today in which rank and open racial prejudice is allowed to reign supreme. Though often called the sport of gentlemen, all too often golf courses, clubs, and tournaments apply the ungentlemanly and un-American yardstick of race and color in determining who may or may not compete." He also criticized President Dwight D. Eisenhower for belonging to the Augusta National Golf Club which limited membership to Caucasians only.(10)

Robinson was particularly exasperated by the treatment of Charlie Sifford and Ted Rhodes by the PGA. In calling for prompt remedial action he stated: "Not only should court action be considered, but I feel the issue is one for thorough investigation by the Civil Rights Commission." In the same column, he took Bing Crosby to task for not permitting black golfers to participate in the California tournament that bore his name.

When Charlie Sifford finally obtained his "approved player" card from the PGA in early 1960, Robinson congratulated both Sifford and the organization in his column. He also noted that J. Edward Carter, managing director of the PGA, had told Sifford that Robinson's criticisms of the organization in his newspaper columns had played a role in the final decision. Later in 1960, Robinson praised New York State Attorney General Louis Lefkowitz for insisting that an invitational tournament on the Cornell University golf course be open to all upper New York state club professionals. Aware that public pressure was mounting, Robinson also stated that " . . . there are growing signs that the days of the PGA's bias clause will have to be numbered if it expects to continue as a national regulatory agency."(11)

In 1962, Robinson participated in the annual Ray Mitchell North-South Tournament held in Miami, Florida. In his column after the event, the former baseball player commented on the favorable changes he had observed in racial attitudes since he first went to the city to start spring training 15 years earlier. Racial barriers in places of public accommodation had disappeared, and he praised Miami's City Manager for the courteous treatment accorded to the black golfers and their guests.

The following year, Robinson once again leveled criticism at network television by blistering the producers of "All Star Golf" and "Challenge Golf" for not featuring any black golfers. On the basis of Charlie Sifford's performance, Robinson argued in his column, he should be featured in one of the televised matches. Jackie then urged blacks to boycott the products of sponsoring companies. His last sentence summarized his militant approach to the situation. "Let's give our champions some real backing by refusing to support businesses which choose to ignore our existence."(12)

Within days after the column appeared, Robinson was contacted by an advertising agency representing one of the sponsors. After offering a tortuous "explanation" of its position, the sponsoring company agreed to give Sifford favorable consideration for the next television season if he remained a PGA contender. In his printed response, Robinson congratulated the company for its sensitivity but was careful to point out: "We beg for nothing. We ask no special

Two of the greatest African American athletes in history, Jackie Robinson and Althea Gibson, compared scores while competing in the 1962 North-South golf tournament in Miami Springs.   (Credit: Bettmann Archives)

privilege. We seek merely adjustment by men of good will to equalize the injustices practiced by those of bad will."

Despite his celebrity status, Robinson was not immune to the indignities perpetrated on African Americans by certain members of the golf world. In 1966, he and a business partner filed a lawsuit charging that they were discriminated against when they attempted to buy a country club in upstate New York. On another occasion his application for membership in a private country club near his home in Stamford, Connecticut, was rejected because some members feared he would attempt to participate in the club's social events.(13)

Robinson continued to be an active golfer and an activist for the game until he lost his vision due to the ravages of diabetes. In 1972 he suffered a fatal heart attack, and his illustrious life came to an end.

Billy Eckstine

Best remembered as a jazz vocalist and band leader, Billy Eckstine is decidedly less well-known for his support of black golf. Eckstine's connections with black golf would have remained obscure, in fact, had Charlie Sifford not included an important section on Eckstine in his book *Just Let Me Play*.

William Clarence Eckstine was born in Pittsburgh, Pennsylvania, on July 8, 1914. He played the piano and sang in a church choir during childhood but was more interested in playing football. After completing high school in Pittsburgh, he received a sports scholarship and entered a preparatory school in Virginia with the intention of pursuing a career in physical education. When he broke his collarbone playing football, Eckstine decided to switch to singing. A few years later, he was hired to be the principal vocalist for the Big Band of Earl "Fatha" Hines. Eckstine stayed with Hines for four years, then had his own band from 1944 to 1947. The consummate entertainer, Eckstine was greatly admired for his singing, dancing and trumpet-playing.

In the early 1950s, Eckstine hired Sifford to be his personal assistant and golf instructor. His pay was $150 a week and road expenses. With a young family to support, Sifford appreciated the steady salary and the sense of security that enabled him to practice and play across the country. In addition to providing Sifford with a regular income, Eckstine (commonly referred to as "Mr. B") often gave Sifford entry fees for tournaments. On at least one occasion, Sifford remembers that "Mr. B" gave financial assistance to Ted Rhodes as well. In 1957, Sifford decided to leave Eckstine to try his luck on the circuit. "Mr. B" knew that the time had come, and he wished Sifford well.

Eckstine loved to play golf and took his clubs with him whenever he went on an engagement. He played with most of the top black golfers and was thoroughly familiar with the difficulties they encountered in trying to get sponsors. In 1961, in one of his few public statements on golf, the singer urged fellow golfers to boycott manufacturers of golf equipment who failed to sponsor African American professionals.(14) In his book, Charlie Sifford recognized the unheralded but valuable assistance he received from Eckstine. "To have a man like Mr. B behind me was the most wonderful thing that ever happened to me. He was the benefactor who made it possible for me to live my dream."

Billy Eckstine died on March 8, 1993, at the age of 79.

Moss H. Kendrix

Although many details of his personal life are unavailable, there's enough known about Moss Kendrix to conclude that he was a strong supporter of black golf.

He was probably born in the southern part of the U.S. toward the close of World War I. By his own account, he began caddying at the age of twelve. Later, he attended Morehouse College in Atlanta, Georgia, and was a member of the school's first golf team.(15) Sometime around the end of the second World War, Kendrix moved to Washington D.C. and established a public relations firm. For many years, the Coca Cola Company was his main client. Additional business relationships included Carnation Milk and a Miami automobile franchise. At a time when corporate America was not inclined to provide funds for black golf events, the gregarious Kendrix used every ounce of his persuasiveness and charm to convince prospective clients that they would reap dividends from any support they rendered.(16)

In addition to successfully promoting many organized events, Kendrix was instrumental in gaining support for the United Golfers Association, Western States Golf Association, and the North-South tournaments. Locally, he obtained support for the Capitol City Open and the YMCA Open. From the 1950s through the 1970s, one could count on seeing Kendrix's face in photographs taken at black golf events. An even-tempered, well-dressed man who enjoyed great popularity in the black community, Kendrix had his office at Eleventh and U Street in Washington and was visited frequently by many of the important black golfers of the day.

In the late 1950s, Kendrix began writing a guest column for *Tee-Cup*—the official organ of the Western States Golf Association. In the latter half of 1959, he assumed the position of editor-publisher in a brief, but unsuccessful, attempt to revitalize *United Golfer*, the UGA's official publication. At one time during the early 1960s it was rumored that he contemplated becoming a professional golfer, but there is no evidence that he ever did so.

The later years of Moss Kendrix have gone unreported, and attempts to trace his subsequent whereabouts and activities have been unsuccessful. This is unfortunate because Kendrix had high hopes for the future of black golf. It would be interesting to learn whether he continued to feel that way.

Within a decade after the end of the second World War there were telltale signs that the existing black golfing events were insufficient to satisfy the growing demands of players. With rising expectations and greater disposable incomes, this new generation wanted access to better golf courses and wanted to stay and eat at first-class establishments. Those living in the northern part of the country were eager to get a mid-winter break from the icy blasts and go to places where they could not only play golf but also enjoy the sun, sand, and surf. Consequently, it was only a matter of time before individuals with vision would recognize that there were financial and recreational rewards to reap by tapping this burgeoning market.

Ray Mitchell

After the end of World War II, Raymond Page Mitchell came to the realization that black golfers had a pent-up desire for additional opportunities to play. He was convinced that a midwinter tournament would be welcomed and that southern Florida was admirably suited for such an event. It had not been attempted before, and although he realized that there would be pitfalls before it became a reality, he was willing—in fact, eager—to accept the challenge.

Born on February 10, 1907, in Jacksonville, Florida, Mitchell was one of five children raised by a widowed mother. He started caddy-ing at the age of twelve, working at two of the municipal golf courses until he completed high school. In 1924 he took a job on a coastal steamer sailing between Jacksonville and New England ports. Before he had completed his first trip, Mitchell left the ship in New York harbor and decided that this was the city where he wanted to settle. Later that same year he married Thelma Broner, a transplanted Georgian. In 1926, their first child, Beverly, was born.(17)

Shortly after the birth of Beverly, Ray obtained employment as a redcap (and sometimes Pullman porter) working at New York City's Pennsylvania Station. Over time, he became friendly with William Willis, club manager at Shady Rest Golf & Country Club in Scotch Plains, New Jersey, and the two men organized a series of Sunday tournaments that proved to be popular during the summer months. In the early 1950s, Mitchell retired from his job at Pennsylvania Sta-tion and started the Famous Golf School in Harlem. Through his golf lessons and his experience with the Shady Rest tournaments, Mitchell made a number of contacts which would later prove help-ful. The golf school also staged tournaments, and that only added to Ray's expertise.(18) All the while, he continued to nurse his cher-ished idea of starting a midwinter event.

In 1954, after a series of false starts, the first annual Ray Mitchell North and South amateur and professional golf tournament was held in Jacksonville. The initial event was so successful that a black physi-cian in Miami persuaded Mitchell to move the following year's event from Jacksonville to Miami. Within a few years the annual Ray Mitchell event began to attract golfers from across the country. The Schaefer Brewing Company became a leading sponsor, and through Mitchell's contacts with Joe Louis, Jackie Robinson, Sugar Ray Robinson, and the ever-present Moss Kendrix, the tournament se-cured the sponsorship of the Coca-Cola Company.

About this time, Mitchell began to encounter the first of a series of obstacles. He was informed by many of his prime sponsors that they planned to reduce their contributions to his event so that they could spread their funds among more recipients. This prevented Ray from providing purses to the professional golfers. Another major re-versal came in the mid-1960s when he was informed by Miami offi-cials that he would not be allowed to use his name in the official title of the event. From then on, it was known as the North-South Tournament. Eventually, though, sponsors returned and professionals began playing once again for cash prizes. Despite requests from many quarters, however, the official tournament name remained the North-South Tournament.

These annual tournaments were not only important golf events, they were enormously popular social affairs. Over the years, they attracted top golf pros such as Ted Rhodes, Charlie Sifford, Zeke Hartsfield, Renee Powell, Pete Brown, and Althea Gibson. Well-known amateurs included Ann Gregory, Joe Roach, Joe Louis, and Ralph Dawkins. Entertainers, athletes, and politicians came to see and be seen, and it was not unusual for as many as 300 businessmen and professionals to attend the event.(19) Continuing into the late 1990s, the event founded by Ray Mitchell must be regarded as part of a vital historic legacy. When he died in 1974, a few months after the devastating loss of his beloved daughter and confidante, Beverly, Raymond Page Mitchell had established a tradition that will occupy a hallowed place in the institutional memory of black golf.

Earl Jackson

Born on August 24, 1924 in Farmville, Virginia, Earl Jackson caddied as a youngster on a hometown golf course. After graduating from high school, he attended Morehouse College in Atlanta before entering the U.S. Navy in 1942. During the war he saw service as a boatswain's mate first class aboard a patrol boat in Alaskan waters. Jackson was discharged from the Navy in 1946, and two years later joined the New York City Police Department. An unusual appointee for that period in New York City history, Jackson was one of the few African Americans selected for assignment to the prestigious motorcycle division. The quintessential tall, dark, and handsome man-about-town, Jackson was an imposing figure as he sped about the city in his natty uniform astride a shiny motorcycle. On one of his patrol assignments, Jackson had a chance encounter with an owner of a midtown travel and tour organization called "Blue Cars." As a result of that meeting, he became a part-time salesman for the company and it ushered in the start of a new career.

An avid golfer since his caddying days, Jackson and a friend went to Puerto Rico in 1954 for a short golf vacation. While there, the two hit on the idea of trying to arrange a tournament in the Caribbean.(20) Not in a position at the time to pursue the concept further, the two let the idea lay dormant. Shortly after the Puerto Rico jaunt, Jackson became president of the Guardians Association, an organization of African American members of the New York City Police Department. In 1956, continuing his part-time association with Blue Cars, Jackson arranged for some 70 fellow police officers to spend 30 days in Europe studying police procedures and sightseeing. The tour was a great success and it convinced Jackson more than ever that blacks were eager to travel and could afford first-class tours.

Over the next few years, Jackson continued arranging small tours. By 1962, he was ready to launch the pet project he had conceived with his friend eight years earlier. With Jackie Robinson and football legend Jim Brown as celebrity participants, Jackson believed he could convince at least 50 people to sign up for a Puerto Rico golf tour. As it turned out, more than 200 people participated. Jackson could now substantiate his long-held assumptions about the potential in the black golf-travel market. A year earlier, he had established a small business—International Golf Tours (IGT)—which he operated from an office in his home. With the experience from the first successful golf tour, Jackson was confident enough to sever his business relations with Blue Cars and operate independently.

Jackson's dynamism and leadership qualities were also recognized by his superiors in the police department. In 1962, he was promoted to the rank of detective sergeant. Benefiting from management courses offered to its officers by the police department, the ex-motorcycle cop continued to arrange golf tours in his spare time. By 1967, no longer able to continue the hectic pace required to handle what had become two full-time jobs, Jackson retired as a law enforcement officer. He could now devote all of his energies to the travel agency.

Shortly after his retirement from the police department, Jackson moved IGT to an office building near his home in the borough of Queens, New York, and the staff was gradually expanded. By 1971, Jackson had taken a group of 250 golfers to Sweden, and had arranged tours (golfing and nongolfing) to the Caribbean, Europe, and Latin America. That same year, IGT was featured in a magazine article as one of the largest black travel agencies in the country, with annual gross earnings in excess of one million dollars.(21) An industrious individual who combined personal magnetism with a thoughtful approach to entrepreneurship, Jackson persuaded the Pepsi-Cola Company to be a sponsor of the golf tours. This new business arrangement made it possible for IGT to charter a jumbo jet for a 1973 tour of the African continent. Much of Jackson's subsequent success was due to the network of well-known and respected contacts he'd established in the black golf community, both domestically and abroad. Among the group of area representatives he recruited were Bill Dickey (see Chapter 11), James Morrow, and Franklin Lett, Sr.

In 1979, IGT took a group to Paris for several days of golf and sightseeing.(22) Always on the alert for new opportunities, Jackson also traveled to the Far East. In Australia, he was approached about the possibility of golf tours "Down Under." On one other occasion, it was rumored that Eastern Air Lines was considering him for a senior executive position. Unfortunately, by 1982, the stressful nature of his daily business routine began to exact a toll. On February 1, 1983, Earl Jackson died in New York City.

In his lifetime, the former Virginia caddy had demonstrated his business acumen and used the skills he had developed to open new vistas for black golfers.

Figures in the Shadows

Until the mid- to late-1960s, when illicit drug traffic began to rampage around the world, one of the characteristics of larger black communities in the United States was the presence of a small group of individuals, most commonly male, who lived at the margins of the law. In some situations they combined legal activities with those that were either questionable at best or downright unlawful at worst. Some, for example, owned small hotels, saloons, or poolrooms, but were also involved with the numbers racket, gambling, loan sharking, and/or bootlegging. For the most part they shunned violence, preferring to evade the law with wile and deception. Yet, when they saw fit, they could be ruthless with those who ran afoul of them. Most had not gone beyond high school, but often they were shrewd money managers who, under different circumstances, might have become successful in legitimate business. Their business activities usually took place late at night or in the early morning hours, leaving them with sizable amounts of idle time during the day. It was an ideal situation for many of them to become involved with golf. Often heavy gamblers, they might lose or increase their winnings from an all-night poker session or from betting sprees on the golf course the following day—and vice versa.

A few had caddied during their youth, but most had not. What they had in common was a passion for the game and the opportunities for wagering. In addition, some of them began to develop an interest in talented younger golfers who aspired to make a career of professional golf. As time passed, it was not unusual for one of the members of this shadowy element to become a "silent" benefactor or sponsor of a struggling professional. The assistance ranged from outright cash to payment for dental expenses; from car loans to the purchase of new golf clubs; from hotel bills to transportation tickets. As might be expected, they preferred (indeed, insisted) on remaining anonymous.

Despite their existence at the periphery of society, it's clear they played a role in the emergence of some of the better black golfers. They are worthy of mention as part of the varied texture of African American golf history.

Helping Hands Across the Racial Divide

Considering the enormity of the task they faced, it is not surprising that the numbers of white men and women who supported black golf were small. Those who "dared," however, demonstrated a strong sense of fair play by standing firm against the prevailing current of bigotry and racial discrimination in the mainstream golf world. None were motivated by considerations of personal gain. On the contrary, because their positions were unpopular, they ran the risk of public criticism and ostracism. Long before black golfers could rely on legal remedies to redress their shabby treatment, their only hope lay with this enlightened handful of the white population.

Mention was made earlier of Theodore Havemeyer's ruling at the second U. S. Open that permitted John Shippen to play; of the principled position taken by Interior Secretary Harold Ickes to desegregate the public golf courses in Washington, D. C.; and of the courageous stand of California Attorney General Stanley Mosk against the PGA. Also recounted was the instruction provided to Joe Bartholomew by golf course architect Seth Raynor, and choral leader Fred Waring's trust in Dewey Brown to assume the managerial reins at his Shawnee-on-the-Delaware resort. In each instance, a white advocate acted on the basis of what was right rather than what was expedient.

Charles "Chick" Evans, Jr., winner of the 1916 U. S. Amateur and U. S. Open, as well as a four-time member of the U. S. Walker Cup team, was a close friend of African American football legend Frederick Douglass "Fritz" Pollard. As youngsters they caddied together at a local Chicago golf course and were teammates on neighborhood baseball and football teams. In 1922, Evans provided a substantial loan so that Pollard could start an investment firm.(23)

Chick Evans never capitalized on his golf successes and insisted on remaining an amateur. Nor did he forget his humble origins. He maintained a deep attachment to caddies throughout his lifetime, and in 1930, in conjunction with the Western Golf Association, established a college scholarship program for deserving caddies. Over the years some 85 scholarships have been awarded to African Americans. In an article in the June 28, 1941, issue of the *Saturday Evening Post*, Evans recalled that after winning the 1916 U. S. Amateur, his mother told him to use some of his newly-acquired fame to improve the lot of caddies. Because he had won the Amateur using golf clubs made by Dewey Brown, and because of his close association with Fritz Pollard, Evans felt strongly that due consideration should be given to the educational needs of African American caddies in his scholarship program. He made certain that they were not overlooked.

It may have seemed that way, but Evans' "voice" was not the

only one crying out in the wilderness. Organizers of present-day golf tournaments have benefited considerably from the inventiveness and showmanship of George Storr May, majority stockholder and long-time president of Tam O' Shanter Country Club on the outskirts of Chicago. For a millionaire business executive, May entertained a number of working-class views that differed sharply with those of many colleagues in the private sector. He also recognized the folly of racial discrimination. May's promotional activities for his tournaments were regarded with contempt by the conservative elite who held sway over the culture of pre-World War II golf tournaments. For the first Tam O' Shanter National Open in 1941, May offered an unheard-of large purse, slashed the price of admission, threw open the clubhouse doors, installed indoor and outdoor slot machines, staged a water extravaganza in the club's swimming pool, and at strategic holes, erected grandstands that were equipped with loudspeakers to broadcast the results of events taking place elsewhere on the course. In one magazine article, the tournament was ridiculed as "a cross between a country fair and an airplane crash."(24)

For the 1942 event, May went even further. He increased the prize money, maintained low admission prices, urged patrons to travel to the site by streetcar, and, for what was billed as a first in golf history, announced that there would be a professional tournament and an amateur tournament going on at the same time. May was now described as "the inventor of the jumbo double dipper tournament at bargain prices." When he subsequently announced that African Americans golfers would be allowed to enter, the descriptions of George May were not so nice. Many people felt he had committed the ultimate and unpardonable act of heresy.

Earlier that year, when seven black golfers were barred from the Hale America tournament in Chicago, it provoked the ire of Benjamin A. Grant, African American alderman of the Windy City's third ward. In addition to threats of legal action, Grant, an enthusiastic golfer himself, sent telegrams of protest to the mayor and U.S. military officials. Grant also wired George May. The exchange of correspondence is reproduced in its entirety because of its importance to the historical record.

George S. May
2600 North Shore Avenue
Chicago, Illinois

On behalf of the Negro citizens of Chicago and all believers of fair play, I take the liberty of asking your attitude toward participation of Negro golfers in the $15,000 Tam O' Shanter National Open and All-American tournaments to be held at Tam O' Shanter C. C. in July for benefit of Army Emergency relief. I hope you will agree that Negroes, who stand ready to do all in their power to aid America's war effort including, of course, service in the armed forces should have an opportunity to aid in the worthy cause which you are promoting and to compete against other entrants in the Tam O'Shanter tournaments on the basis of merit alone.

Benjamin A. Grant

Within a few days, May sent his reply:

May 27, 1942

Alderman Benjamin A. Grant
103 East Forty-seventh Street
Chicago, Illinois

Dear Mr. Grant:
I have received your wire in which you request a statement of my attitude toward the participation of Negro golfers in the $15,000 Tam O' Shanter National Open and the All-American Amateur golf tournament to be held at the Tam O' Shanter Country Club here from July 20 to 26.
In answer I would like to point out that the words "National" and "All-American" in the names of these tournaments mean exactly what they say. These tournaments are open to any American who is willing and able to qualify under the rules of competition which have been set up for all participants.
I am fully aware that Negroes are being called upon, to-

gether with peoples of every race, color and creed, to do their full share in the national war effort and I know that many thousands of your people are presently serving with the country's armed forces. Private Joe Louis comes to mind in this connection as an outstanding example of all-around good citizenship. I can see no reason, therefore, why they should not contribute their services on an equal basis with everyone else in such patriotic sports events as the Tam O' Shanter tournaments, which, as you know are being staged for Army Emergency Relief. Their participation will not only be permitted at the Tam O' Shanter tournaments, it will be welcomed.

> Sincerely yours,
> George S. May
> President
> Tam O' Shanter
> Country Club(25)

To implement May's forthright stand, a citizen's committee was established to select suitable black candidates for invitation to the qualifying rounds. Despite predictions to the contrary, the Tam O' Shanter events proved to be highly successful fund raisers during and after the war. When the events were discontinued in 1958, it was noted that "Not only was May's tourney the richest in the history of golf, but it was the most liberal. More Negro golfers have competed in the Tam O' Shanter than any other tournament in the world."(26) Over the 17 years of its existence, the names of African American participants in Tam O' Shanter events read like a "Who's Who" of black golf. Among those who competed were Ted Rhodes, Ann Gregory, Joe Louis, Charlie Sifford, Thelma Cowans, Howard Wheeler, Zeke Hartsfield, Calvin Searles, Pat Ball, and John Dendy. If the white golf establishment had had the courage and common sense to follow the praiseworthy example of George Storr May with regard to its racial policies, American golf could have been spared years of anguish, embarrassment, and contention.

Even though most instances of racial discrimination in golf involved all-male organizations, male officials and male players, women's golf was not spared from the virus of racism. Fortunately, however, there was a small cadre of white women golf enthusiasts who did not shy away from doing battle against racial bigotry. In early 1944, after many years of seeking unsuccessfully to become affiliated with the all-male PGA, a group of white women decided to form their own organization. A draft charter for the constitution was prepared and circulated among interested female golfers. In the draft were clauses stipulating that "playing professionals shall be white women" and "teaching professionals shall be white women." Almost immediately, former Women's World Champion Betty Hicks took exception to the exclusionary clauses. At the time, Hicks was serving as a commissioned officer in the U. S. armed forces and " . . . she believed that the fight against discrimination was one of the things the war was all about."(27) Obviously, her protestations were heeded. When the Women's Professional Golf Association (WPGA) was chartered in December of 1944, the objectionable clauses had been removed.

Another racial episode in women's golf occurred during the civil rights era of the 1960s. The LPGA at this time was anxious to expand its tournament circuit by playing on courses that were part of newly-built private housing communities. During this period, both Althea Gibson and Renee Powell were playing on the LPGA tour and real estate developers feared their presence at tournaments would make the new housing communities less desirable for prospective white home-buyers. Borrowing a trick from the PGA, two sponsors decided to designate their tournaments as "invitational" events. By doing so, they could eliminate Gibson and Powell from participation. Learning of the plan, LPGA tournament director Lennie Wertz told the sponsors that "We all play or we all stay away."(28) Because the players supported Wertz's decision, the LPGA later failed to obtain some tournament dates in the South. The organization had, however, demonstrated its resolve by refusing to surrender to the forces of racial intolerance.

Charlie Sifford probably has played with more top white professional golfers than any other American of African descent until the advent of Tiger Woods. In his book *Just Let Me Play*, Sifford mentions a dozen or more white fellow professionals who always treated him with courtesy and respect. Jimmy Demaret, Gary Player, Dave Hill, Ed "Porky" Oliver, Jack Nicklaus, and Bob Rosburg are among those singled out by Sifford. Moreover, on the book's dust jacket, gracious comments about Sifford are made by Tom Watson, Arnold Palmer, Gene Littler, Mike Fetchik, and Don January.

Recounted earlier were the positive feelings that Bill Spiller expressed for Frank Stranahan, Lawson Little, and Sam Snead. During her years on the LPGA tour, Renee Powell was befriended by Canadian Sandra Post, 1968 winner of the LPGA championship. In addition to Lee Trevino and Gary Player, Lee Elder recalled the helpfulness of Ben Crenshaw and Dave Stockton. Now more than fourscore years old, long-time pro Johnny Bulla remembers the enjoyment he derived from being paired with a black golfer at the 1944 Tam O' Shanter.(29) There's no doubt that a number of other white professional golfers could be added to this impressive list.

The world of professional golf is a microcosm of the beliefs, attitudes, and perceptions of the greater society. Yet within that insular world there have been sensible men and women who understood the precepts of the late Reverend Martin Luther King, Jr. and were prepared to accept others on the "content of their character rather than on the color of their skin." Others remain trapped within the confines of ignorance, envy, and stereotypes. The situation within the ranks of professional golf has improved considerably since the end of World War II, and most palpably within the last 25 years. As the nation's demographics continue to change, it should be obvious even to the most obtuse that those changes will be reflected in the ethnic composition of professional golf. Will it adapt and follow the exemplary conduct of such notables as Jimmy Demaret, Betty Hicks, Bob Rosburg, and Sandra Post? Or will it have to be dragged kicking and screaming into the twenty-first century? This, of course, is a question that transcends the golfing community and deserves serious consideration by society as a whole.

10 | Adding Up the Score

To reflect on the history of African Americans and the game of golf is to engage in an absorbing intellectual exercise. The saga is a small but revealing part of the human drama that began with the transatlantic slave trade. As such, it adds an important dimension to the wider history of black Americans. Before attempting a brief summary of all that has taken place in the romance between African Americans and golf, it is worthwhile—some might say essential—to mention certain items that were either omitted in earlier chapters or received limited emphasis. Mainly, these items relate to specific categories of black golfers who are a vital fraction of the total number. The other items are concerned with a few discrete sets of activities. All are part of the black golf landscape, and when juxtaposed to issues, personalities, and events presented earlier, this final body of information becomes an integral part of the historical mosaic.

"Modern" Professional Golfers

Like their white counterparts, most black professional golfers live in relative isolation from the rest of society. The demands of constant practice, travel, and income uncertainties are stressful, and frequently lead to an abandonment of aspirations for a career in professional golf. Black professionals, while no longer exposed to the gross humiliations of bygone years, still encounter resistance when they try to

168

obtain positions as club professionals. The very small number of young black male golfers who are in the professional pipeline is a matter of concern. The situation for women may be a bit more hopeful, but even here the outlook should be tempered with caution.

A review of the historical record since the "Caucasian only" clause was removed from the PGA constitution in 1961 reveals that one of the more noteworthy developments has been the number of African American professional golfers who have demonstrated the highest levels of ability. Beginning with Charlie Sifford's victory at the Hartford Open in 1967, several black players have proved to even the most obstinate skeptic that they have earned the right to compete.

Charlie Sifford

According to the 1997 Media Guide of the PGA Senior Tour, Charlie Sifford's "special interests" are music and boxing. He was born on June 2, 1992, in Charlotte, North Carolina. Charlie started his career in golf as a caddie, and began playing professionally at the age of seventeen on the old UGA Tour. He won the Negro National Open six times. He joined the PGA Tour in 1960. In 1967 he won the Greater Hartford Open for his first PGA victory. Two years later he won the Los Angeles Open in a play-off with South African Harold Henning. Other victories include the 1957 Long Beach Open, the 1963 Puerto Rico Open, the 1971 Sea Pines Open (a satellite event), and the 1975 PGA Seniors Championship. In 1980, Charlie began playing on the brand-new PGA Senior Tour. His Senior wins include the 1980 Suntree Classic and the three titles he captured with partner Roberto De Vicenzo at the Liberty Mutual Legends of Golf. Moneywise, his biggest years were 1985 ($104,294) and 1989 ($96,340). His career earnings on the regular PGA Tour were $341,344. Since playing the Senior Tour, Charlie has won $927,790. Sifford and his wife, Rose, had two children and live in Kingwood, Texas. Charlie's autobiography, *Just Let Me Play*, was published in 1992.

Charlie Sifford playing in the 1969 Los Angeles Open, a tournament which he won in a sudden death playoff to capture the $20,000 first place check.   (Credit: Bettmann Archives)

Pete Brown

Peter Brown was born on February 2, 1935, in Port Gibson, Mississippi. He turned professional in 1954, and won the Negro National Open in 1961 and 1962. Pete began playing on the PGA Tour in 1963. A year later, he became the first African American to win a PGA event when he won the Waco Turner Open. Over the 18 years he played the regular tour, Brown finished among the top-60 money winners three times. His best year was 1970. He won the Andy Williams San Diego Open that year and finished 35th on the money list. His money total for his PGA Tour career, which ended in 1985, was $221,966. Between 1985 and 1991, Pete played 76 events on the Senior PGA Tour. Three times he finished in the top-10, but he never won. His total Senior Tour money was $108,221.

Lee Elder

Robert Lee Elder will always be known for being the first African American golf professional to play in The Masters in Augusta, Georgia. He was born in Dallas, Texas, on July 14, 1934. Like a lot of black golfers, Elder learned the game as a caddie. For a while he caddied at Pebble Beach Golf Links in California. After turning pro in 1959, he played whenever and wherever he could. Much like his

A 39-year-old Lee Elder celebrates after winning the 1974 Monsanto Open.
It was the first PGA victory by an African American man since 1969.
(Credit: AP/World Wide Photo)

friend Lee Trevino, Elder gained a reputation as a golf "hustler." In 1967 Lee won 18 of the 22 UGA tournaments he entered. Late in 1967 he joined the regular PGA Tour. In 1968—his first full year on tour—he received national attention at the American Golf Classic in Akron, Ohio. Tied with Jack Nicklaus at the end of the event, Elder battled the Golden Bear in a sudden-death play-off before losing on the 5th hole. Six years later, Lee won the Monsanto Open—again in a play-off—for his first victory. This historic win qualified him to play in The Masters the following spring. Lee won the Houston Open in 1976, and the Greater Milwaukee Open and American Express Westchester Classic in 1978. His career prize money on the regular tour was over $1,000,000. In 1979, Elder was a member of the U.S. Ryder Cup team. He joined the Senior PGA Tour in 1984, and won eight tournaments in a four-year span. His best earnings year as a Senior was 1985 ($307,795), when he won four times. Following the 1990 season, health problems began to plague the popular pro. In 1996 he was forced to withdraw from five of the last eight Senior Tour events. Lee's combined earnings from his play on both tours totals over $2,500,000. He lives in Pompano Beach, Florida.

Cal Peete

Calvin Peete was born in Detroit, Michigan, on July 18, 1943. While still a youngster, Cal broke his left elbow in a fall and it prevented him from fully straightening his arm. He left school at an early age and eventually began making a living by selling goods to migrant farm workers. At the encouragement of friends, Cal took up golf in 1966 at the "old" age of 23. Five years later, he turned pro. Four years after that, Cal successfully completed the PGA Tour qualifying school and began playing the circuit full-time. His first victory came at the 1979 Greater Milwaukee Open. Between 1982 and 1986, Cal won 11 more tournaments, including the '86 Tournament Players Championship. That prestigious victory earned him a 10-year exemption on the PGA Tour. Amazingly, considering his long-ago injured elbow, he won the Tour's driving accuracy title 10 consecutive years (1981–1990). Cal won the Ben Hogan Award (for overcoming illness or injury) in 1983, and the Vardon Trophy (for low scoring average) in 1984. In '83 and '85 he was a member of

Calvin Peete lining up a putt on the Senior PGA circuit.
(Credit: Allsport)

the U.S. Ryder Cup team. After 1986, Cal was slowed by back and shoulder problems and, consequently, enjoyed little success. Through 1993, however, he had earned over $2,300,000 on the PGA Tour. He turned fifty that same year and soon began playing on the Senior PGA Tour. As of 1997, Cal had not won a Senior event. That year Cal earned $160,025. He and his wife, Pepper, live in Ponte Vedra Beach, Florida, and have six children.

Jim Thorpe

Jim Thorpe was born on February 1, 1949, in Roxboro, North Carolina, the ninth of twelve children in his family. A talented enough high school running back to earn a football scholarship to Morgan State University, Thorpe also excelled at golf. He became a golf professional in 1972 and qualified to play on the PGA Tour full-time in 1975. Thorpe was unable to earn enough money during the 1976 season to secure his playing privileges but requalified at the 1978 Tour School. Thorpe's first PGA Tour victory came at the 1985 Greater Milwaukee Open, and his second came at the Seiko Tucson Match Play Championship that same year. At the '85 Western Open, he achieved something of a dubious distinction by losing the title in a play-off with amateur Scott Verplank. In 1986 Thorpe won again at the Seiko Tucson Match Play Championship for his third and last PGA Tour victory to date. Jim's highest earnings year was 1985 with $379,091. A wrist injury caused him to miss most of 1988, but he regained his form and played steadily through 1994. Since that time, Thorpe has played sparingly on the regular Tour. Through 1997, his career earnings were just under $2 million. Jim and his wife, Carol, have two children and reside in Buffalo, New York. He will reach the requirement age for the Senior GA Tour in 1999.

Charles Owens

As a youngster, Charles taught himself to play golf by hitting bottle caps with a tree branch. Like a lot of self-taught African American golfers, he swung his clubs cross-handed. A good all-around athlete as a youth, Charles earned a football scholarship to Florida A&M

University. As a 6'3" tight end, he was good enough at the game to earn a tryout with the Cleveland Browns. Before he was drafted into the NFL, though, he was drafted into the U.S. Army during the Korean War. Assigned to the 82nd Airborne Division, Owens suffered a shattered left knee during a training jump and that was the end of his hopes of playing football. His knee had to be fused in the fully extended position. In the mid-'60s, after numerous operations and after not playing golf for 15 years, he took up the game again. In 1967, he turned pro. In 1970 he began playing when he could on the regular PGA Tour. His physical problems, plus poor putting, caused him to only win about $16,000 in seven years on tour. Switching to the Senior PGA Tour in 1981 (and eventually to a new 50-inch putter), it only took him about three years to earn about the same amount. In 1984, Charles won over $15,000. In 1985, he won almost $93,000. The next year, he won two tour events and over $225,000 in total money. After 1992, he played the tour sparingly. His total earnings on the Senior Tour were $793,362. Charles is a member of the Florida Sports Hall of Fame, and was the recipient of the prestigious Ben Hogan Award in 1987.

Jim Dent

James Lacey Dent was born on May 9, 1939, in Augusta, Georgia. As a younger man, Jim caddied at both Augusta National Golf Club and Augusta Country Club. He became a golf professional in 1966, and joined the PGA Tour in 1970. Dent was winless during his 19-year career on the regular tour, but won a total of $565,245. His best year was in 1974, when he won over $48,000. Since joining the Senior PGA Tour in 1989, Jim has won over $5,000,000 and has taken eleven titles, including two in his first season. In 1990, Dent won four events and finished sixth on the money list. In 1994, he won over $950,000. Known for being an extremely long driver of the golf ball, Jim is also a die-hard fisherman. He was inducted into the Georgia Golf Hall of Fame in 1994. Jim and his wife, Willye, had two children of their own. In 1994, the Dents adopted a baby son. The following year, they adopted a baby daughter. The family makes its home in Tampa, Florida.

Walter Morgan

Another player on the Senior Tour from Georgia is Walt Morgan. He was born in Haddock, Georgia, on May 31, 1941. Growing up, Morgan's first love was baseball, not golf. Like Cal Peete, Morgan didn't take up the game until he was in his twenties (the first time he played, he shot a 79). Walt spent 20 years in the U.S. Army—including two tours in Vietnam. In 1975 and 1976 he won the All-Service golf championship. He left the military in 1980, attempted to qualify for the PGA Tour, but missed by one stroke. Morgan spent the next 10 years as a club pro in Texas before turning fifty. He then successfully qualified for the PGA Senior Tour. Since playing the senior circuit, Walt has won three times (twice in 1996). In 1996 he earned $848,303. In '97, although winless, he earned nearly $696,000. In 1995 he was elected to the North Carolina Black Hall of Fame. Walt and his wife, Geraldine, have two children. They make their home in Ponte Vedra, Florida.

Bobby Stroble

Unlike Walt Morgan, fellow Georgian Bobby Stroble did play on the regular PGA Tour—although sparingly and with little success. Like Morgan, Bobby enjoys fishing in his spare time. He was born on December 4, 1944, in Albany, Georgia. He turned professional in 1967 and made his debut on the regular tour in 1976. Bobby's lack of success on the regular tour forced him to play a limited schedule on the Nike Tour during 1990-1991. For the next three years, he got his game ready for the Senior PGA Tour by playing in Senior Series tournaments. In 1994 Stroble was the leading money-winner of that satellite tour, with over $85,000. Bobby joined the Senior Tour in 1995 but only played in three events. In 1996 he played in 35 events and won almost $465,000. Bobby won almost 312,000 in 1997 but it was not enough to prevent him from having to re-qualify for the Senior Tour. Unfortunately, Bobby did not retain his full-time status for 1998. He and his wife, Natalie, live in Miramar, Florida. They have two children.

    None of these golfers requested or received any special dispensations in order to achieve; all they sought was a level playing field.

With the exception of a single comment, this author intends to resist the temptation to add to the millions of words that have been written to extol Tiger Woods, that incredibly talented young man from Cypress, California. It is my belief that even if he never wins another tournament, his place in golf history is unequivocally and absolutely assured by his amateur and professional records to date.

Golf Instructors

From the earliest days of the sport's existence, there have been those who were prepared to render solicited and unsolicited advice on ways to improve one's playing ability. In more recent times, many black instructors were also top-notch players in their own right. Because of restrictions that governed PGA membership, however, they could not obtain formal certification and were forced to become self-declared instructors—their reputations spread by word-of-mouth. Few, if any, became wealthy from teaching. For most of them, then *and* now, it was a matter of love and respect for the game combined with a desire to share their knowledge with others.

James "Jimmy" DeVoe and Pat Ball were two black instructors who were well known in the years after the first World War. Both had played in the first UGA tournament in 1926, both were respected golfers, and both were praised by their pupils. DeVoe, born in Michigan in 1888, was initially based in New York. He moved to the Los Angeles area in the 1950s. Ball spent most of his life in Chicago.

Another well-known golf instructor was Lucius Bateman. He was born in Louisiana shortly after the turn of the twentieth century, but grew up in Biloxi, Mississippi. After learning the game through caddying, he was selected by the professional at Edgewater Hotel and Country Club in Biloxi to be his instructional assistant. Following a stint in the Air Force that ended in 1941, "Loosh" Bateman moved to San Francisco where he worked in the shipyards for four years. At some point, Bateman started teaching at a driving range. He taught there for more than a quarter of a century and secured the respect and admiration of thousands of golfers in the Bay Area. Former British Open champion Tony Lema was one of his star pupils.

Another highly-acclaimed black golf instructor—particularly in the Detroit area—is E. (Earlon) Ben Davis. Known far and wide as "Ben," he was born in Pensacola, Florida, in 1912. He moved to Detroit in 1933 and has lived there since. He started giving golf instructions in 1936 and over the years has taught a wide range of prominent citizens. Joe Louis was one of his star pupils at one time and Davis, together with Bob Seymour, conceived the idea of establishing the Joe Louis Open golf tournament. The "Brown Bomber" wholeheartedly endorsed the proposal and for a number of years the tournament was a popular event on the black circuit.

A member of the PGA since 1969, Davis retired in 1972 after 36 years on the tee at Detroit's Rackham Golf Course.

Other well-known black golf instructors were James Jackson at Van Cortlandt Park Golf Course in New York City; Joseph Hampton (recently retired) at the Ted Rhodes Golf Course in Nashville, Tennessee; and the recently deceased Willie "Barracuda" Jefferson, who for many years was a fixture at Langston Golf Course in Washington D.C.

Although the author was unable to determine exactly how many African Americans have been golf instructors, it would not be surprising if there were several hundred. Their contributions to African American golf history are obvious.

Black Golf Halls of Fame

Since the end of World War II, three golf Halls of Fame have been established to recognize those who have contributed to the development of black golf. The first was the brainchild of Anna Robinson of the Chicago Women's Golf Club. Although sources differ about the year it was founded, the UGA Hall of Fame most likely came into existence in 1959. However, it did not receive official approval from the UGA until 1977. In the late 1970s, a campaign was undertaken to develop an institutional base for the Hall of Fame at the Afro-American Museum and Cultural Center in Wilberforce, Ohio. Unfortunately, the efforts fell on hard times and those involved were unable to secure sufficient funds to complete the project.

It is estimated that since it first came into existence, nearly 100 individuals have been inducted into the UGA Hall of Fame. As best as can be determined, all of the inductees have been African Americans.

A second Hall of Fame was established in 1976 by the Western States Golf Association (WSGA). Spearheaded by Frederick H. Horton, then president of the organization, the WSG Hall of Fame inducts three individuals every two years. Those honored are members "who have served the Association with Dignity, Dedication and Honor."

The third such body, the National Black Golf Hall of Fame, was founded in 1986 by Harold Dunovant, a long-standing black golf professional. Based in Winston-Salem, North Carolina, one of its goals is "to honor anyone who has done the most to promote golf in the black communities." Because it is open to anyone who meets the qualifications, regardless of race, color, or creed, both Arnold Palmer and Gary Player are among the nearly 100 people who have been inducted into the NBGHOF in its more than 10 years of existence.

Black Golf Publications

First published in 1936, *United Golfer* was the official UGA organ and the first black golf publication with a substantial readership. It was a casualty of the war years and attempts to revive it during the early 1960s were unsuccessful.

Tee-Cup, the official publication of WSGA, appeared in late 1955 or early 1956. J. Cullen Fentress, WSGA president at the time, was the driving force behind the publication. Probably because Fentress was himself a printer, *Tee-Cup* was noted for the excellent quality of its print and the clarity of the photographic reproductions. Of the early publications mentioned, it is the only one still in existence.

Presumptive evidence suggests that the magazine *On The Ball* first saw the light of day about 1958. Although the words "Coast To Coast" appeared on its masthead, the magazine tended to focus on East Coast (primarily New York City) golf activities. The departure of *On The Ball*, despite its somewhat regional focus, left a void that has not been filled.

Minority Golf is the latest publication to address African American matters. A quarterly publication, the first issue appeared in late 1995.

Beginning with the spring 1996 issue, *Tee-Cup*—though still wholly owned by WSGA—has been published within the pages of *Minority Golf.*

Although not strictly periodicals, souvenir programs are available at many of the tournaments that are held each year. Examples are those printed for the annual East/West Classic, the annual Morehouse College Invitational Tournament, the Wake-Robin annual tournament, and the WSGA annual tournament. These publications often contain valuable articles on African American golf history.

Black Golf Organizations

Of the many factors that influenced the course of African American golf history, few were of greater significance than the role of the United Golfers Association (UGA). After it came into existence in 1926 (or thereabouts), it served many important functions. It gave black golfers a collective sense of identity; it helped to shield black golfers from the hostility of mainstream golf; it attempted to stimulate the formation of junior golf programs; it was an agent of social bonding; and it supported efforts to end racial discrimination in the sport. In short, the UGA was the organizational base and psychosocial anchor of the African American golfer. At its peak, it was the center of black golfing expression. As time passed, the UGA demonstrated an ability to survive numerous challenges, due in great measure to effective leadership by many of the elected officials. As a result, it enjoyed the trust and confidence of the membership. Had it not existed, black golfers would have been without a true institutional friend.

The UGA, nevertheless, had its weaknesses which apparently were intractable. It is difficult to state with precision when the UGA began to lose its position of preeminence in black golf. Available evidence suggests that the decline started in the mid-1970s. At that time, the organization had achieved its peak membership, estimated variously from 30,000 to 100,000. Indications that there was trouble afoot, some subtle, others more obvious, began to appear with increasing frequency. Fewer UGA events received attention in the sports pages of black newspapers. During the prime years of the organization, a prominent feature of the annual tournament was the professional competition that was held over a three-day span. In later years, the professional competition was gradually reduced to a one-day event.(1) By 1975, the professional competition segment of the annual tournament ceased to exist. Over time, smaller groups began to stage tournaments to satisfy the growing appetite of the African American community.

With the wisdom and infallibility of hindsight, it is relatively easy to enumerate a host of other structural problems that worked to erode the UGA's strength and influence. To begin with, the UGA was never a truly nationwide organization. Its membership was concentrated in the Midwest and on the East Coast. There were some affiliated groups in the South but, for the most part, the South and the rest of the nation were outside the UGA orbit. Periodic rumors of financial mismanagement—even if unfounded—was another recurrent problem that tended to undermine confidence in the leadership. Failure to establish a permanent headquarters and an administrative infrastructure compromised efficient handling of day-to-day affairs. As the leadership changed periodically, papers were shifted among new groups of officials, inevitably leading to the misplacement of documents, correspondence, and other types of organizational material. These managerial inadequacies adversely affected communication with the membership.

To some degree, this problem might have been minimized if the UGA had not discontinued publication of its organ, *The United Golfer*. As a result, the organization had to rely on the souvenir programs for the annual tournaments to inform the membership of internal developments. Also, without a regularly published organ it was difficult to let members know about issues and events in the broader world of golf that affected black golfers. In fact, only the annual tournament and tournament-related activities offered tangible benefits to the membership. Disappointing also was the UGA's failure to forge links with other black sports organizations. A glaring example of this isolationism occurred in 1962 when the (black) American Tennis Association scheduled a *golf tournament* during its annual championship. There is no evidence that the UGA played any role in the event.(2)

Perhaps the greatest stumbling block faced by the UGA was the dilemma posed by bittersweet "victories" in the struggle for racial integration. To this day, the issue is a conundrum for black organizations and institutions. What is the price for assimilating into the mainstream and, as a corollary, has the price been too high for the returns? Some organizations, such as the NAACP, the National Urban League, the American Tennis Association, and the Historically Black Colleges and Universities have opted to retain their ethnic identities and have survived. Others, such as the Negro Baseball League, made different choices and withered away.

African American essayist and literary scholar Gerald Early provides an interesting perspective on the phenomenon. Looking at what happened in baseball, Early believes that "When integration came to professional baseball, it was a one-way street. The major leagues could steal black players from the Negro leagues . . . but the Negro leagues could not steal players because they lacked the economic resources, the organizational strength and the prestige to do so." Although the situations were not identical, there were similarities in the problems faced by the UGA in the post-civil rights era and those of the Negro baseball leagues after Jackie Robinson's arrival in mainstream, organized baseball. "In the end," Early writes, "owners of black baseball clubs had no choice but to endorse integration because it was what both the black players and the black people wanted."(3)

Troubled by internal weaknesses and compelled to confront powerful forces in the dominant culture, the UGA was unable to stem the decline in its membership and influence. It lost its vigor, dynamism, and popular appeal. To date, a suitable alternative or replacement has not been found.

One disappointing feature of the last decade is the minuscule number of black golfers on the regular PGA Tour. Other than the phenomenal Tiger Woods, the only other player is Thorpe . . . and *he'll* be moving to the Senior Tour in 1999. Concerted efforts are required to develop young black golfers, such as Martin Roache and Adrian Stills, who can withstand the rigors of qualifying school and make it to the tour. A similar situation exists in women's professional golf. Currently there are *no* African American women on the LPGA tour. It is hoped that La Ree Pearl Sugg and Nikia Davis will rise to the challenge.

A *positive* development in the last 10 years has been the proliferation of small tournaments aimed at attracting black amateur golfers. Primarily fund-raisers for a variety of causes, these events are staged by college and university alumni associations, civic organizations, local golf groups, civil rights organizations, and business groups. According to information compiled by the Sports Opportunity and Information Center in Richmond, California, 167 of these tournaments were scheduled in 1995. By the following year, the number had risen to 194. The total seems destined to increase each year until well into the next century. Because it is difficult to obtain accurate information, it is believed that the numbers cited significantly under-represent the actual number of annual black golf tournaments. The true numbers may be three or four times greater. In conjunction with the proliferation of tournaments, there has been a parallel rise in the number of black golfers—male and female. Unfortunately, reliable numerical or demographic data on black golfers is unavailable.

11 | Building the Pipeline: Youth and College Golf

Interest in the golfing activities of black youngsters is not a recent phenomenon. As far back as 1928, a sportswriter for the Pittsburgh Courier reported on two brothers who traveled from Steubenville, Ohio, to Pittsburgh to play in a junior tournament at the Schenley Park Golf Course. Although they had mediocre scores, the writer praised Herman and Cornelius Bass because it was the "first time any golfers of color have entered a white tourney, or in fact any tourney in Pittsburgh." Recognizing the need to stimulate the game among black youth, a national interscholastic tournament was started in 1940 to coincide with the Southern Intercollegiate Golf Tournament.(1) The tournaments were played at the Tuskegee Institute golf course, but they were discontinued in 1944 because of World War II. After the war was over, the high school tournaments were not resumed.

One of the great postwar disappointments has been the failure to develop strong golf programs for the young black population. In great measure, it accounts for the small number of African American golfers currently on the major professional tours. There are many reasons for the sad state of junior golf in the black community and they have been well known for a long time. Nearly a quarter of a century has passed since the problem was discussed in the now-defunct magazine *Black Sports*.(2) Mentioned in the article were such familiar factors as the expense involved, absence of well-financed

training programs, the "glamour" of other sports, aggressive and se-
ductive recruiting practices in the other sports, the legacy of racial
discrimination in golf, and the failure to expose black youth to golf
at an early age. By no means exhaustive, the list of reasons that was
compiled is as valid today as it was when the article first appeared.

The arrival of Tiger Woods on the golf scene, however, has added
a new dimension to junior golf. But it would be unfair to place the
burden for improving minority junior golf solely on the shoulders of
young Mr. Woods, as large as they might be. Likewise, it would be
unrealistic to believe that the mere presence of this remarkably talented golfer will be the panacea for correcting years of indifference
and apathy. Thus far, Tiger Woods has shown a sincere commitment
to doing what he can to encourage minority youngsters to take up
the game, and there is every reason to believe that he will continue
to do so. His assistance will be of enormous value, but it should not
be regarded as a substitute for the combined efforts of parents,
school athletic officials, corporate sponsors, golf organizations, and
other interested parties. To think otherwise is to run the risk of
watching another quarter-century roll by without any material betterment of the state of minority junior golf.

The previously mentioned 1973 article in *Black Sports* was equally
perceptive in its treatment of the situation in college golf. Compar-
ing it to junior golf, the author stated: "The college picture is not
much brighter. It can't be without high schools feeding the colleges
good young Black golfers." While it is possible to name a Lee Carter,
Jr., who played golf at the University of New Mexico; a Mark
Brown, who was an important member of the Yale University golf
squad; or a Andy Walker of the Pepperdine College golf team,
African American students on the golf teams of predominantly white
institutions of higher learning are generally few in number.

Of necessity, therefore, the record of golf among black college and
university students is essentially what has taken place at the Historically Black Colleges and Universities (HBCUs). When such HBCUs
as Florida A & M University in Miami, Florida; South Carolina State
College in Orangeburg, South Carolina; and Bethune-Cookman
College in Daytona Beach, Florida, were established in 1887, 1896,
and 1904, respectively, each had large, vacant expanses of campus.
Members of the faculty, student body, and administration often used

these tracts of vacant land for golf practice.(3) As the years passed, three- and four-hole "courses" were fashioned on the property using "do-it-yourself" methods. In 1926, nine-hole courses were opened at both Wilberforce University in Xenia, Ohio, and at Tuskegee Institute in Tuskegee, Alabama. In 1938, thanks to the efforts of Tuskegee Athletic Director Cleveland L. "Major" Abbott, Tuskegee's golf course was the site of the first HBCU Intercollegiate Golf Tournament. With the exception of four years during the World War II period (1944–1947), the event was held on the 3,400-yard, par-35 Tuskegee course until 1980.(4)

Despite the difficulties, concerned groups across the nation continue to search for ways to provide opportunities in golf for black youth. In most cities with sizeable black golf populations, there are one or more programs designed to lure black youngsters away from the so-called traditional sports. Usually coupled with some type of scholarship incentive, these programs encourage youngsters to complete a college education while improving their skills on the golf course. Attracting elementary and junior high school students is often more problematic because tangible incentives are not always easy to provide.

In the spring of 1987, the National Minority Golf Scholarship Fund began to provide academic scholarships to minority students and financial support to a group of predominantly minority institutions of higher learning for strengthening their golf programs. Fundraising efforts center around separate but simultaneous college and celebrity tournaments in Cleveland, Ohio, during the month of May and a benefit concert held on Labor Day weekend. By 1997, the Fund was able to provide scholarships to all of the 15 participating institutions. To accommodate greater demand, in 1998 the PGA will host the Fund's national collegiate golf championship at the award-winning PGA Golf Club, The Reserve, located near Port St. Lucie, Florida. Cleveland will continue to be the site of the celebrity tournament.(5)

Perhaps the best-known program for introducing golf to minority youth, and arguably the most successful, is offered by the National Minority Junior Golf Scholarship Association (NMJGSA). Founded in 1984 and based in Phoenix, Arizona, the organization is directed by William "Bill" Dickey, a retired realtor and insurance broker.

Born in Collingdale, Pennsylvania, on the outskirts of Philadelphia, Dickey moved to Phoenix in 1952 and began playing golf in 1958.

Described as someone who " . . . has formed more civic-minded groups than most people join in a lifetime," Dickey developed the vision for a minority youth golf program in the 1970s. In 1983, a year before NMJGSA was formally incorporated, the embryonic organization held its first golf fund-raiser, the East/West Golf Classic. At the initial event, 132 golfers participated and $1,500 was raised. By the next year, proceeds had more than tripled and the new organization awarded scholarships to four college-bound students.(6) In 1997, 288 golfers participated and scholarship awards were expected to be in excess of $110,000. Total scholarship awards since 1984 have exceeded a half-million dollars, disbursed to some 500 students.

The annual East/West Golf Classic enjoys the reputation of being the foremost golfing event of its kind in the black community, and it is actively supported by individuals, organizations, and businesses across the country. By the end of 1997, NMJGSA was expecting to announce its formal merger with the recently established National Minority Golf Foundation (NMGF). Under the new arrangement, the older organization will continue to operate the annual East/West Golf Classic and provide scholarship assistance. NMGF, on the other hand, will concentrate on strengthening current golf programs at HBCUs, working to create wider business and employment opportunities for minorities in the golf industry and cooperating with other groups to develop internship training programs for minorities.

Though caution is needed when attempting to predict the ultimate outcome of efforts to enhance the golf outlook for African American youth, whatever success is achieved is due in part to the commitment of Bill Dickey, the patron *nonpareil* of minority junior golf. In recognition of his notable contributions to black golf—particularly in the realm of junior golf—Dickey was inducted into the National Black Golf Hall of Fame in 1989.

A 1995 survey of 84 Historically Black Colleges and Universities provided some interesting information. At the time of the survey, it was learned that 22 HBCUs had golf teams. Responses from 18 of these teams revealed that:

- 157 students participated
- 76% were male; 24% were female
- 74% were African American; 21% were Caucasian; 19% were Hispanic; 6% belonged to other ethnic groups
- 72% of the HBCUs provided golf scholarships; 33% were for full tuition; 17% were for partial tuition; 28% provided a combination of full and partial tuition (five institutions declined to provide information on this question)
- Seven of the responding HBCUs had all-female golf teams
- None of the institutions owned a golf course

In late 1997, two new programs were announced that were designed to open the game to more minority youngsters. The first is an initiative of the World Golf Foundation and is designated as The First Tee. The list of individual and organizational supporters is impressive. The program's thrust is to foster the development of facilities where participants can learn the game. A primary objective is the establishment of 100 golf facilities with a combined capacity of introducing 1,000 individuals to the game each year.

A second program, For the Good of the Game, was also announced recently by the United States Golf Association. Planned to last over a 10-year span, the USGA program is pledged to spend $50 million in support of projects that will place golf within the reach of all Americans.

Both programs are long overdue and if they fulfill their expectations, they could help significantly to increase the pool of younger minority golfers.

Epilogue

Adaptability to change is one of the characteristics of humankind from time immemorial. The African taken forcibly from the shores of the Motherland to the Western hemisphere was no exception. Under trying circumstances, the newcomer learned languages unrelated to his native tongue; new foods were prepared and eaten; new religious beliefs and rituals were absorbed and practiced. Whether it was in the ballet or on a battleship, becoming an astronaut or grafting an artery, learning to play croquet or using a compass, skiing or stockbrokering, the historical record is clear and unequivocal. The African American tried to the utmost to participate in all areas of human endeavor, and some excelled in the process. That applied to golf as it did to everything else. Certainly there were blacks who caddied, but that was not their sole involvement with the sport. As the African American golf experience becomes more widely known, the world will recognize the many contributions African Americans have made to the game. African Americans are here to stay.

And they will continue to play and compete on fairways that were once forbidden.

Notes

Chapter 1

1. Donna Wyant Howell, comp., *I Was a Slave*. (Washington, D.C.: American Legacy Books, 1995), 35.
2. H.B. Martin, *Fifty Years of American Golf.* (New York: Dodd, Mead & Company, 1936), 49.
3. *Sport in America,* edited by David K. Wiggins (Champaign, IL: Human Kinetics, IL, 1995) 144–145.
4. *The Daily Plant,* City of New York Parks & Recreation, 10 (July 7, 1955).

Chapter 2

George Grant

1. In later years, the family home became one of the way stations of the Underground Railroad that was established and operated clandestinely to enable fugitive slaves to escape to the northern United States and Canada. Guil Jones, "Historically Speaking: Dr. George F. Grant," *Black Sports,* July 1973, 12–13.
2. Biographical sketch of George F. Grant by George Washington Forbes, undated. Typed manuscript in the Boston Public Library, Department of Rare Books and Manuscripts. Ms. Am., 282 (16), RBD 437.
3. An undated handwritten entry by Frances Grant in her father's papers deposited in the Beinecke Rare Book and Manuscript Library at Yale University reads, "getting a house—difficult then as now for a Negro . . ."
4. Taped interview with Frances Grant by Robert Hayden, circa 1974.
5. Barbara Blossom, "Golfer Once Pined for Pastures," *Reminisce,* May/June 1995, 19.
6. United States Patent Office. George F. Grant, of Boston, Massachusetts. Golf Tee. Specification forming part of Letters Patent No. 638,920, dated December 12, 1899. Application filed July 1, 1899, Serial No. 722,500. (No model).

7. Wornie L. Reed, "Who Invented the Golf Tee?" *Trotter Institute Review*, Fall 1991, 21.

Walter Speedy

8. "Local Gossip." *New York Age*, May 19, 1988, 3.
9. "Walter Speedy, Pioneer Golfer, Dies Suddenly," *Chicago Defender*, December 4, 1943, 11.
10. "Colored Golf Players," *New York Age*, October 14, 1915, 6.
11. "Weak Petitions Stops Golf Club Injunction," *Chicago Defender*, September 3, 1927, 1.
12. "Golf," E.L. Renip, *Chicago Defender*, July 16, 1921, 10.
13. "Windy City Golf Kings Invade East," *Chicago Defender*, September 1927, 9.

John Shippen

14. Frank Strafaci, "Forgotten Pioneer Professional," *Golfing*, March 1957, 11.
15. Philip St. Laurent, "The Negro in World History—John Shippen," *Tuesday* magazine, April 1969, 17.
16. Entry for John Shippen; Sheet 35, Line 16, Enumeration District 7, District of Columbia Census of Population; (National Archives Microfilm Publication T742, Roll 7): Tenth Census of the United States 1880; Records of the Bureau of the Census, Record Group National Archives, Washington D.C. The date is confirmed in "The Family Recollections of Beulah Shippen and Mabel S. (Shippen) Hatcher," a privately printed and copyrighted genealogical memoir prepared by Paul E. Sluby, Sr., 1994, p. 37.
17. *The Ministerial Directory of the Presbyterian Church in the United States of America*, Edgar S. Robinson, Ed., Vol. 1 (Oxford, OH: Ministerial Directory Company, 1898), 478.
18. Averill D. Geus, *Maidstone Club: The Second Fifty Years* (West Kennebunk, ME: Phoenix Publishing, 1991), 98.
19. Peter F. Stevens, "In the Eye of the Storm," *Golf Journal*, 40 (June 1966), 12–15.
20. Golf. *Outing's Monthly Review*, 31 (October 1897), 88.
21. *Fifty Years of the Maidstone Club: 1891–1941* (East Hampton, NY: The Maidstone Club, 1941), 108. In addition to the error about Shippen's racial ancestry, this pejorative statement concerning Native Americans suggests that the golfer had a drinking problem.
22. R.H. Smith, Jr., "The Oldest Homebred Pro in America," *United Golfer and Other Sports*, 3 (1938), 3.

23. E. Digby Baltzell, *Sporting Gentlemen* (New York: The Free Press, 1995), 152.

24. Ralph Wise, correspondence with author on December 5, 1996, and telephone interview by author on December 7, 1996. When he was twelve years old, Wise began caddying for Shippen at Shady Rest and at other golf courses in New Jersey and New York. Fittingly, in 1993 he posted a score of 64 to win the third annual John Shippen Memorial Golf Tournament.

25. Alberta Shippen, telephone interview by author on August 15, 1995. No longer living, Ms. Shippen was the daughter-in-law of golfer John Shippen and had been married to his son, William Hugh Shippen.

26. Thurman P. Simmons, Sr., personal interview by author on November 2, 1996, and telephone interview by author on December 7, 1996. Simmons is chairman of the John Shippen Memorial Foundation, Inc.

Joseph Bartholomew

27. Accounts of Bartholomew's age differ. The author relies on information provided by Bartholomew's daughter during a telephone interview on August 8, 1995.

28. Interview with Henry Thomas, December 12, 1995. A long-time golf professional in New Orleans, Thomas was a white friend and colleague of Bartholomew.

29. M.R. Werner, "Joe Bartholomew Never Had Time to Read Horatio Alger," *Sports Illustrated* (Southern Edition), 25 (July 18, 1966), S5–S7.

30. Ed Tunstall, "N.O. Hall Picks Four," *New Orleans Times-Picayune*, January 28, 1972.

Dewey Brown

31. Editors, "Dewey Brown: Superintendent, Professional, Gentleman," *Golf Superintendent*, (July 1974); 31–34.

32. Roland Brown, Dewey Brown's son, telephone interviews with author on June 19, and November 20, 1995.

33. Herbert B. Graffis, *The PGA* (New York: Thomas Y. Crowell), 1975.

Chapter 3

1. Lewis Hine, *Kids At Work* (New York: Clarion Books, 1994), 32.

2. Throughout the research, the author has not been able to identify one African American female caddie.

3. Wilbur Young, "No Golfer's a Hero to His Caddy; But Many Would Be Easy Victims," *New York Amsterdam News,* August 17, 1940, 15.

4. Unnamed author, "Yes Sir, J.C. Can Hit That Golf Ball: Rockville Gets Long Hitting Citizen." *United Golfer And Other Sports,* 3(1938), 11.

5. John R. Tunis, "Caddy Crisis," *New York Times Magazine,* June 8, 1952, 56.

6. Dewayne Wickham, *Woodholme* (New York: Farrar, Straus & Giroux, 1995), 73–74.

7. Unnamed former caddie, personal interview by author at Joseph M. Bartholomew, Sr. Municipal Golf Course, New Orleans, LA, on December 11, 1995.

8. Joseph Hall, active caddie, personal interview by author at Congressional Country Club, Potomac, MD, on December 30, 1996.

9. Jaime Diaz, "The Men the Masters Forgot," *Golf Digest,* April 19, 1993, 132–139.

Chapter 4

1. Edward Kimble, *The Blackberries and Their Adventures* (New York: R.H. Russell, 1897), 43.

2. Emmett J. Scott, [1920] 1969 *Negro Migration During the War* reprint, with new preface by Thomas R. Cripps. New York: Arno/*The New York Times.* Scott was a golfer, and in the 1920s he served briefly as president of the National Capital Country Club outside Washington, D.C.

3. "Pankin (*sic*) Wins at Golf," *New York Age,* November 11, 1915, 5.

4. "Swastika Golfers Win," *Pittsburgh Courier,* September 3, 1932, Section 2, 4.

5. "Walter Speedy, Pioneer Golfer, Dies Suddenly," *Chicago Defender,* December 4, 1943, 11.

6. "The American Tennis Association," Bertram L. Baker, undated typescript. For some 30 years, Baker served as executive secretary of the organization.

7. Marvin P. Dawkins, "African American Golfers in the Age of Jim Crow," *Western Journal of Black Studies,* 20, no.1 (1996): 39–45.

8. John S. Gordon, "The Country Club," *American Heritage,* 41, Sept–Oct. (1990): 75–84.

9. "Only Negro Golf Course in U.S. Is Thriving in Suburban Jersey," *New York Sun,* July 11, 1922, 11.

10. Lawrence J. Londino, *A Place for Us.* Partial text of Dr. Jeffrey Sam-

mons from a videotape produced by the Elder Sports Management Institute (Palm Beach, FL: Professional Golfers Association, 1995).

11. Jonathan Z. Larsen, "Tulsa Burning." *Civilization,* 4, Feb.–Mar. (1997): 46–55.

12. "Mapledale Country Club, Boston Resort," *Pittsburgh Courier,* July 30, 1927, Section 1, 10.

13. "New England Resort Changes Hands," *Pittsburgh Courier,* March 23, 1929, Section 1, 2.

14. Emma Lue Sayers, "Famous Parkridge Club Purchased by Wealthy Negroes," *Pittsburgh Courier,* May 8, 1928, Section 2, 1.

15. Michael Winerip, "His Most Powerful Drive Was to Play, with Pride," *New York Times,* June 28, 1996, Section A, 14.

16. Sabrina Jones, "Black Families in Franklin Open Golf Club," *Raleigh News and Observer,* October 11, 1996, Section B, 5.

Chapter 5

1. "Hotel Dale, Cape May, N.J." *New York Age,* May 18, 1911, 5.

2. Bill White, "In and Around New York," *Chicago Defender,* December 24, 1921, 10.

3. William de Hart Hubbard, "The Color Line," *Pittsburgh Courier,* December 12, 1925, 12.

4. "Fore," *Chicago Defender,* June 25, 1927, Sec. 1, 9.

5. "Eastern Golfers Set for Big Title Tourney," *Chicago Defender,* June 28, 1930, Sec. 2, 5.

6. "Eastern Golf Club—Organized 1932." *Souvenir Programme of the Eastern Golf Association,* 1932, 5.

7. *Colored American Cavalcade,* 35mm, 1 hour 20 min.(?) 1948. Distributed by Sack American Enterprises, Inc. Available for viewing in Motion Picture Section, Library of Congress, Washington, D. C.

8. F.A. "Fay" Young, "The Stuff is Here," *Chicago Defender,* September 10, 1938, 10.

9. "For the Good of Golf," *Chicago Defender,* June 29, 1940, 22.

Chapter 6

The Armed Forces and Black Golf

1. Marvin E. Fletcher, "The Black Soldier Athlete in the United States Army, 1890–1916," *Can. J. History Sports Phys. Ed.,* 3 (December 1972), 16.

2. Herbert B. Graffis, *The PGA* (New York: Thomas Y. Crowell), 1975.

3. Joe Burlas, "A Soldier's Story," *Soundoff*, November 10, 1994, 10. In 1950, Guillory won the UGA National Amateur Championship and, after retiring from the army, he became the golf instructor at Walter Reed Army Medical Center in Washington, D.C.
4. John Hope Franklin and Alfred A. Moss, Jr., *From Slavery to Freedom*, 7th ed. (New York: McGraw-Hill) 1994.
5. Major Leroy Williams (USMC, Ret.) January 22, 1996 response to a questionnaire sent by the author.

Two Postwar Black Titans of the Golf Links

1. Accounts of the birthdate of Rhodes vary by as much as six years. The year 1913 was selected because it is the date that appears on the plaque installed by the Nashville Metropolitan Board of Recreation and Parks at the Rhodes Golf Course in Nashville, Tennessee, and is corroborated by his daughter.
2. "Joe Louis Open $1,000 Top Prize to Ted Rhodes," *Chicago Defender*, August 30, 1947, 11.
3. Charlie Sifford, *Just Let Me Play*, (Latham, NY: British American, 1992).
4. Russ J. Cowans, "'Made Mistake' PGA Secretary Tells Teddy," *Chicago Defender*, August 20, 1949, 15.
5. Lillian Scott, "Joe Defeated in First Round of Amateurs," *Chicago Defender*, August 6, 1949, 19.
6. "No Color Line," *Golf World*, January 25, 1952, 8.
7. John Bibb, "Elder Recalls Ted Rhodes' Fatherly Help," *Nashville Tennesseean*, July 16, 1969, unpaginated.
8. Ruby Wheeler (Mrs. Howard Wheeler) telephone interview with author on April 15, 1996.
9. "Negro Open," *Time*, September 12, 1938, 35.
10. Joel W. Smith, "Down the Fairway," *Atlanta Daily World*, August 17, 1941, 8.
11. Keith Wimberly, "Lady Luck Was with Show," *Chicago Defender*, January 22, 1938.
12. "Howard Wheeler Wins Joe Louis Open Title," *Chicago Defender*, August 4, 1951, 20.
13. Cloyte Murdock, "Howard Wheeler Focuses Eyes on 1952 National," *Chicago Defender*, June 30, 1951, 19.

Chapter 7

1. Library of Congress, Prints and Photographs Division. Call No. LC-D4-18479.
2. E.L. Renip, "Golf," *Chicago*, August 13, 1926, 10.
3. Arthur P. Davis, *From the Dark Tower*, Washington, D.C.: Howard University Press, 1981.
4. Courtland Milloy, "For Black Women, Golf Wasn't Easy," *Washington Post*, April 26, 1987, B3. The quoted statement was made by Karen Jefferson, then senior manuscript librarian at Moorland-Spingarn Research Center, Howard University, Washington, D. C.
5. "Local Women's Golf Club Has First Banquet," *Baltimore Afro-American*, April 30, 1938.
6. Memorial Program For "Walter Speedy Day," sponsored by the Chicago Women's Golf Club, August 19, 1945.
7. "Mrs. Wilson in Tam O'Shanter," *Chicago Defender*, August 26, 1944, 7.
8. "Louis 'Ups' Golf Monies; Bars Gals from Playing," *Chicago Defender*, May 31, 1947, 11.
9. Thelma McTyre, "Along the Fairway," *Chicago Defender*, March 12, 1949, 14.
10. Lucy Bond interview with author on January 6, 1995.
11. JoAnn Overstreet, telephone interviews with author on March 11, 1997; March 24, 1997; April 12, 1997; and May 5, 1997. Overstreet is Ann Gregory's only child.
12. "Midwest Golf Title is Won by William Douglas, Gary," *Chicago Defender*, August 4, 1945, 7.
13. "Down the Fairway," *Chicago Defender*, July 29, 1950, 18.
14. Russ Cowans, "Golf Experts Believe Ann Gregory is Greatest of the Women Champs," *Chicago Defender*, October 14, 1950, 18.
15. "The Social Side of Golf," *Sepia*, 11 (September 1962), 53.
16. Rhonda Glenn, *The Illustrated History of Women's Golf*. Dallas, TX: Taylor Publishing, 1991.
17. "Down the Fairway," *Chicago Defender*, October 14, 1950, 18.
18. "Gregory Wins Senior Women's Golf Tourney," *Gary Post-Tribune*, undated and unpaginated.
19. Audra D. Strong, "Golfing Champ Keeps Swinging at 76," *Gary Post-Tribune*, July 1, 1989, A1.
20. Edgar Brown was the American Tennis Association (ATA) men's singles champion in 1922, 1923, 1928, and 1929.
21. Timothy Thomas personal interview with author on November 16, 1995.

22. Dr. Elizabeth Brabble personal interview with author on October 8, 1995.
23. Paris B. Brown, "How to Run a Good Tournament," memorandum dated February 21, 1959, Washington, D. C.
24. Ethel Funches personal interview with author on October 8, 1995.
25. Mike Kern, "Keeping Her Charges out of Life's Rough," *Philadelphia Daily News*, July 23, 1993, 10.
26. James Achenbach, "Golf Ambassador Powell Leads by Example," *Golfweek*, January 7, 1995, 5.
27. Jeff Rude, "LPGA Tour Includes First Black Golfer in 17 Years," *Dallas Morning News*, February 18, 1995, A 16.

Chapter 8

1. Ralph Chilton, "National UGA Play to Boston after 16 Years," *Chicago Defender*, August 16, 1941, 23.
2. Bernice Dutrieuille, "Race Golfers Show Up Whites in Law Suit," *Pittsburgh Courier*, August 11, 1928, 1st Sec., 5.
3. "Golfers Sue When Refused Right to Preferred Course," *United Golfer and Other Sports*, 3 (1938), 11.
4. A.M. Wendell Malliet, "Golfing Club Bars Negroes over Protest," *New York Amsterdam News*, June 7, 1941, 1.
5. "Three Golfers Escorted by Police Play a Game," *New York Amsterdam News*, July 5, 1941, 19.
6. Harold Ickes, *The Secret Diary of Harold Ickes*, Vol. 3, *The Lowering Clouds (1939–1941)*, New York: Simon and Schuster, 1954.
7. Frank A. Young, "Hale America Tourney Hitlerizes Seven Golfers," *Chicago Defender*, May 30, 1942, 20.
8. "Par on the Nineteenth Hole," *Golf World*, January 28, 1948, 3.
9. Rowell to Marshall, January 20, 1948, NAACP Collection, Legal File (1949–1952), Container 106, Group B, Library of Congress.
10. "Russ' Corner," *Chicago Defender*, February 16, 1952, 16.
11. Horton Smith, "PGA Stresses 'Guest' Status," *Golf Life*, February 1952, 9.
12. Charlie Sifford, *Just Let Me Play* (Latham, NY: British American, 1992).
13. Spiller to Braverman, January 6, 1960. Courtesy of William Dickey.
14. Bill Plaschke, "He Went Down Swinging," *Los Angeles Times*, February 27, 1997, S2.
15. "Down the Fairway," *Chicago Defender*, August 29, 1953. In the article, columnist Russ Cowans mentions that Spiller and Ted Rhodes stopped in Toledo, Ohio, on their way to a tournament in Montreal.

They had breakfast with Frank Stranahan at his home, then drove Stranahan's car to Canada for the event.

16. *Black Enterprise Supplement*, 27 (September 1996), unpaginated.
17. Wornie L. Reed, "Sports Notes—Blacks and Private Clubs,"*Trotter Institute Review*, 4 (Fall 1990), 17.
18. Ann Gerhart and Annie Groer, "The Reliable Source," *Washington Post*, May 14, 1997, C3.

Chapter 9

1. "Fanfare. Jesse Jackson: Shortage of Black Sportswriters," *Washington Post*, December 13, 1996, B2.
2. Eugene Gordon, "The Negro Press," Annals of the American Academy of Political and Social Science, 140 (November 1928), 248.
3. Floyd J. Calvin, "Lester A. Walton Completes Third Year," *Pittsburgh Courier*, February 7, 1925, 14.
4. David K. Wiggins, "Wendell Smith, the *Pittsburgh Courier-Journal* and the Campaign to Include Blacks in Organized Baseball, 1933–1945," *J. Sports Hist.*, 10 (Summer 1983), 5.
5. Lee Blackwell, "*Defender* Sports Editor Wins Award for Column," *Chicago Defender*, November 26, 1955, 10.
6. "Down the Fairway," *Chicago Defender*, July 1, 1959, 10. The same title was used by Joel Smith for his golf column in the *Atlanta Daily World*.
7. "Sports Front. A Tribute to Golf Writer Frank Lett," *Michigan Chronicle*, May 26, 1973, B1.
8. Sam Lacy, "From A to Z," *Afro-American*, October 30, 1965, 9.
9. Maggie Hathaway response to an August 22, 1996 questionnaire sent by author.
10. Forsett Newby and Ruth Dolores Manuel, "Essence Woman," *Essence*, February 1987, 26.
11. John Glover, "Chip Shots," *Michigan Chronicle*, August 26, 1978, A10.

Joseph Louis Barrow

1. "Joe Louis's (*sic*) Golf," *Golf World*, November 17, 1945, 5.
2. Russell Cowans, "Invite Joe Louis to Mackinaw," *Chicago Defender*, August 5, 1939, 9.
3. Lucius Jones, "Slant on Sports," *Atlanta Daily World*, July 15, 1941, 5.

4. Russ Cowans, "Joe Puts Gloves Down for Clubs," *Chicago Defender*, July 3, 1948, 10.
5. Joe Louis, *Joe Louis: My Life*, New York: Harcourt Brace, 1978.
6. Russ Cowans, "It's Golf Time Now! The Game Has Caught On," *Chicago Defender Magazine*, July 16, 1949, 19.

Jackie Robinson

7. To this day, the late baseball star is criticized by some for what they believe were ill-considered and unwarranted remarks leveled at actor-singer Paul Robeson during testimony Robinson gave in 1949 before the House Un-American Activities Committee.
8. "Jackie Robinson Tells His Story," *Brooklyn Eagle*, August 19, 1948, 8.
9. "Jackie Robinson," *New York Post*, January 27, 1960, 88.
10. The first African American to gain membership was Ronald Townsend, some 35 years after the Robinson column appeared.
11. "Jackie Robinson," *New York Post*, August 24, 1960, 80.
12. Jackie Robinson, "Top TV Golf Shows Snub Professionals of Color," *Chicago Defender*, February 23, 1963, 8.
13. Bill Fields, "Jackie Robinson, Golfer," *Golf World*, April 11, 1997.

Billy Eckstine

14. "Eckstine Raps Golfing Firms; Calls for Negro Boycott," *Jet*, April 20, 1961, 54.

Moss H. Kendrix

15. Moss H. Kendrix, "Be My Guest," *Tee-Cup*, 4 (February 1959), 26.
16. John Hall telephone interview with author on July 16, 1997. At one time, Hall was the assistant tournament director for the Oxon Blades, a well-known golf group in Washington, D.C. During those years he had frequent contact with Kendrix in staging the Capital City Open Golf Tournament.

Ray Mitchell

17. Thelma Broner Mitchell telephone interviews with author on February 22, 1997; June 19, 1997; and July 25, 1997. Ms. Mitchell, Ray's widow, recalled that during the early years of the tournament they were barely able to cover expenses.

18. "Zeke Captures New York City Golf Tournament," *Chicago Defender*, October 11, 1952, 17.
19. "Top Stars in Miami's Golf, Fun 'Classic'," *Chicago Defender*, February 16, 1963, 19.

Earl Jackson

20. James Morrow telephone interview with author on August 19, 1996. A former president of the UGA, Morrow accompanied Jackson to Puerto Rico in 1954 and for a while he was associated with Jackson as an IGT area representative.
21. "Black Travel Agents are Going Places at Last," *Black Enterprise*, June 1971, 16.
22. "Local Golfers are Headed for Paris," *Michigan Chronicle*, February 17, 1979, B2.

Helping Hands Across the Racial Divide

23. John M. Carroll, *Fritz Pollard: Pioneer in Racial Advancement*, Chicago: University of Illinois Press, 1992.
24. Robert M. Yoder and Merle Macbain, "Don't Feed the Golfers," *Saturday Evening Post*, 216 (August 19, 1944), 20.
25. "Negro Golfers Welcomed in $15,000 Open," *Chicago Defender*, June 8, 1942, 19.
26. Russ Cowans, "Tour Tournament Gave Negro Golfers Chance to Compete on Big Time," *Chicago Defender*, April 12, 1958, 9.
27. Elinor Nickerson, *Golf: A Women's History*. Jefferson, NC: McFarland & Co., 1987
28. Rhonda Glenn, *The Illustrated History of Women's Golf*, Dallas, TX. : Taylor Publishing, 1991.
29. Paola Bolvin, "Bulla's Impact Felt on State, U.S. Levels," *Arizona Republic*, June 11, 1997, D1.

Chapter 10

1. Robert Perterson, "Vanishing Almost Before He's Been Seen," *New York Times Magazine*, August 25, 1974, 28.
2. Henry E. Simmons, "ATA Officials Sponsor Golf Tourney at Central," *Chicago Defender*, August 18, 1962, 20.
3. Gerald Early, "Understanding Integration," *Civilization*, 3 (Oct–Nov. 1996), 51.

Chapter 11

1. "College and High School Golf May 8," *Chicago Defender*, April 26, 1941, 23.
2. Robert Guilford, "Opportunities for Young Blacks: What is the Future for Them?" *Black Sports*, 3 (1973), 70.
3. James E. Hawkins telephone conversation with the author on July 30, 1996. Hawkins is the retired Athletic Director at Valley State College, Fort Valley, Georgia, and a longtime official in the Southern Intercollegiate Conference.
4. James E. Hawkins, *History of the Southern Intercollegiate Athletic Conference* (Butler, GA: Benns Printing, 1944).
5. Matthew Huff telephone interview with author on July 7, 1997. Huff is executive director of the National Minority College Golf Fund.
6. "My Home Course," *Golf Journal*, 3 (May 1996), 40.

Appendix A

Noted Black Caddies and Their Patrons

This is an abbreviated list of some of the better-known black caddies with their nicknames (when known) and the names of notable people for whom they provided service.

William Ambrose—John D. Rockefeller
Nathaniel "Ironman" Avery—Arnold Palmer
Jariah "Jerry" Beard—Fuzzy Zoeller
Charlie Carter—Babe Zaharias
Alfred "Rabbit" Dyer—Gary Player, Dave Stockton
Sammy "Killer" Foy—Hale Irwin
Neal Harvey—Lee Trevino
Herman Mitchell—Lee Trevino
Walter "Violence" Montgomery—Julius Boros
Willie "Cemetery" Perteet—President Eisenhower
Willie "Pete" Peterson—Jack Nicklaus
Dale Taylor—Arnold Palmer, Billy Casper, and Dave Hill

Appendix B

Black-Owned Golf Courses

Name	Location	Holes	Existing
Acorn Country Club	Richmond, Virginia	18	No
Apex Golf Course	Atlantic City, New Jersey	9	No
Big Walnut Country Club	Columbus, Ohio	?	No
Booker T. Washington Country Club	Buckingham, Pennsylvania	?	No
Bull Creek Golf & Country Club	Louisburg, North Carolina	9	Yes
Casa Loma Country Club	Power's Lake, Wisconsin	18	No
Cedar River Golf Club	Indian Lake, New York	9	No
Clearview Golf Club	Canton, Ohio	18	Yes
Clinton Park Golf Course	Houston, Texas	9	No
Douglas Park Golf Club	Lexington, Kentucky	?	No
Elizabeth City State University Golf Club	Elizabeth City, North Carolina	9	No
Freeway Golf Course	Sicklerville, New Jersey	18	Yes
Kankakee Shores Golf & Country Club	Kankakee, Illinois	18	No
New Lincoln Country Club	Atlanta, Georgia	9	No
New Lincoln Golf Course	Jacksonville, Florida	9	No
Manaqua Country Club	Amityville, New York	18	No
Mapledale Country Club	Stow, Massachusetts	9	No
Maple Hollow Country Club	Cleveland, Ohio	?	No
Meadowbrook Country Club	Garner, North Carolina	9	Yes
National Capital Country Club	Laurel, Maryland	9	No
Parkridge Country Club	Los Angeles, California	18	No
Rising Sun Golf Course	Ossining, New York	18	No
Riverside Golf Club	Washington, D. C.	9	No
Shady Rest Golf & Country Club	Scotch Plains, New Jersey	9	No
Shangri-La Golf Course	Napanoch, New York	9	No
Silver Rest Golf Course	Glen Allen, Virginia	9	No
Tuskegee Institute Golf Course	Tuskegee, Alabama	9	No

Appendix C

Notable Dates in African American Golf History

Date	Event
December 12, 1899	Dr. George F. Grant awarded patent for first golf tee.
July 25, 1912	Ann Gregory born in Aberdeen, Mississippi.
November 9, 1913	Theodore "Ted" Rhodes born in Nashville, Tennessee.
September 21, 1921	Shady Rest Golf & Country Club organized in Scotch Plains, New Jersey.
April 22, 1937	Wake-Robin Golf Club organized in Washington, D.C.
November 1937 *	Chicago Women's Golf Club organized.
July 23, 1959	William Wright wins National Public Links Championship.
November, 1961 *	PGA removes "Caucasian Race" clause from its constitution.
July 18, 1963	Althea Gibson becomes first African American member of the Ladies Professional Golfers Association (LPGA).
August 20, 1967	Charlie Sifford becomes first African American to win a PGA Tour event (Hartford Open).
April 10, 1975	Lee Elder becomes first African American to compete in the Masters Tournament.
July 11, 1982	Jim Thorpe wins Canadian PGA.
July 11, 1982	Calvin Peete wins Greater Milwaukee Open.
October 9, 1982	Alton Duhon wins USGA Senior Amateur Championship.
October 27, 1985	Jim Thorpe wins Seiko match play championship.
November 2, 1986	Jim Thorpe wins second consecutive Seiko match play championship.
August 25, 1996	Eldrick "Tiger" Woods wins third U. S. amateur championship.
August 25, 1996	Jim Dent wins Bank of Boston Classic.
April 13, 1997	Eldrick "Tiger" Woods, at age twenty-one, wins the Masters Tournament by a 12-stroke margin.

* Exact date not recorded.

Acknowledgments

Some four years ago when I started to explore black golf history, I was not a total stranger to literary research and writing. In my previous professional career I had written biomedical and health-related articles for publication. When my wife was completing her doctoral dissertation and writing the book based on the dissertation, I agonized with her through the lonely hours and sleepless nights. More recently, I shared the anxieties and frustrations of my younger daughter as she successfully weathered the storms of her doctoral studies.

From these personal experiences, it might appear that they would provide adequate preparation to complete this study. Wrong! Even though little has been written, there is a voluminous amount of material on black golf history hidden away in all sorts of places. To bring it to the surface, however, required fairly extensive travel, untold hours spent before the microfilm reader, innumerable telephone calls, and mountains of correspondence. It also entailed a number of tape-recorded interviews and the design and distribution of a golf questionnaire to Historically Black Colleges and Universities.

I was completely unprepared for the overwhelming response I received from people across the country. In addition to letters, faxes, and telephone calls, I was given or loaned clippings from newspapers and magazines, photographs, computer diskettes, scrapbooks, and tournament souvenir programs. It would have been impossible to acquire and sort through the wealth of material without the assistance and cooperation of many, many people. If I omit any of your names, I ask your forgiveness. You may be unmentioned but your generous spirit will never be forgotten.

I cannot adequately convey my profound gratitude to Saundra Sheffer and William "Bill" Dickey for all they have done to help me. With her superb editorial skills and years of experience at the Ralph W. Miller Golf Library, Saundra Sheffer provided incomparable guidance and counsel. Bill Dickey, perhaps the most knowledgeable individual on the status of black golf (past and present), rarely failed to identify a contact or possible source of information. Both Saundra and Bill were mainstays and I shall be forever in their debt.

Repeatedly I called upon Clarence Boyce, Charles Dorton, James Morrow, Timothy Thomas and Dr. David Wiggins. It was enormously reassuring to know that I could rely on their wide breadth of information and eagerness to assist.

I was particularly fortunate to live within close proximity to the Library of Congress (LC) and the Moorland-Spingarn Research Center (MSRC) at Howard University, both located in Washington, D. C. At the LC, Maricia Battle, David Kelly, and Karen Walfall were instrumental in helping me find documentary material in that enormous institution. Marva Belt, Joellen El-Bashir, Kathy Jenkins, Leida Torres, Donna Wells, and Dr. Janet Sims-Wood at the MSRC were always ready to ferret out obscure aspects of black history.

Special thanks are given to librarians, curators, archivists, and support staff at the: Amistad Research Center, Beinecke Rare Books & Manuscript Library, Boston Public Library, California Historical Society, DuSable Museum of African-American History, East Hampton Public Library, Georgia Historical Society Library, Fisk University Library, History Department of the Presbyterian Church, Historic Landmark Committee of Southampton, Lexington Public Library, Massachusetts Public Library, Ralph W. Miller Golf Library, Morgan State University Library, National Afro-American Museum and Cultural Center, New England Historic Genealogical Society, New Orleans Public Library, Penn Center, Sussex County Library (New Jersey), and Carter Woodson Regional Library.

Whenever I sought assistance from the major national golf organizations, I found willing and ready hands at the Ladies Professional Golf Association, National Golf Foundation, Professional Golfers' Association of America, PGA Tour, United States Blind Golfers' Association, and United States Golf Association.

The golf survey of black colleges and universities could not have been done without the able secretarial assistance of Ruth Matthews and Vanessa Stroman-Clay. Ever ready to rescue me from the perverse behavior of my computer were Ms. Joudi Henoud and my son-in-law, Jerome Craig.

A group of helpful individuals were those who granted personal interviews and shared their reminiscences, anecdotes, and impressions with me. In this group I include: Atty. Lucy Bond, Clarence Boyce, Dr. Elizabeth Brabble, W. Cassell Butler, Dr. and Mrs. Walter Combs, Gloria Conway-Jones, Ruth Creech, Ethel Funches, William Gilliland, Martin Guillory, John Hall, Joseph Hall, Rose Harper-Elder, Robert Hayden, Frederick Horton III, Samuel Lacy, Everette Payne, Michael Smith, Pearl Smith, Winifred Stanford, Henry Thomas, Frederick White, and Joe Williams.

An extremely large group of interested individuals provided helpful information by telephone and personal conversation. In some instances as many as eight separate phone calls were made. Among this group were: Dr. Gloria Allen-Toles, Joseph L. Barrow, Ruffin Beckwith, Dr. Joe Beditz, Harold Black, Eugene Boldon, Burl Bowens, Frank Brinkley, Judge Frederick Brown, Roland Brown, T. L. Burns, Dr. John Carroll, Louis Chestnut, Prof. John Henrik Clarke, Hon. James Clyburn (Dem., S.C.), Franklin Coates, W. Paul Coates, Laura Cole, Calvin Cooley, Christopher Davis,

Warren Davis, Dr. Marvin Dawkins, Harold Dunovant, Ms. Billie Duval, Dr. William Edmondson, Ralph Elder, Zollie Gill, Rhonda Glenn, Gregory Gordon, Dr. Debra Newman Ham, Joseph Hampton, Dr. Axel Hansen, Maggie Hathaway, James Hawkins, Dr. William Hayling, Atty. Carl Holmes, Gary Holoway, Alma Fay Horn, Matthew Huff, Gloria Jackson (Mrs. Earl), John Kopera, John Lenear, Franklin T. Lett Jr., Dr. Lawrence Londino, Paul Ludlow, Darrell Macon, Dr. Harry Martin, Herman Mason, Frank Matthews, Atty. Rufus McKinney, Phyllis Meekins, Thelma Mitchell (Mrs. Ray), Dennis Morgan, Earl Nettingham, JoAnn Overstreet, Maurice Patterson, William Phears, Frederick D. Pollard III, Edward Pryce, Louis Rabb, Russell Ravert, Dr. Linwood Rayford, Robert Rickey, Joseph Roach, Lenwood Robinson, Dr. George Rogers, Dr. Jeffrey Sammons, William Seawright, Alberta Shippen, Thurman Simmons, Paul Sluby, Hanno Shippen Smith, Joseph Solomon, William Spiller Jr., Al Stetz, Steven Tate, Michael Thomas, Lawrence Traylor, Robert and Pat Tubbs, Wilbur and Willa Turner, Harold Villere, Ruby Wheeler (Mrs.Howard), Donald White, Peggy White, John Whittiemore, Dewayne Wickham, Leroy Williams, Ralph Wise, Dr. Charles Wright, and Atty. Eric Yeager.

Even with the enormous reservoir of goodwill that greeted me at every turn, my attempts would have been futile without the daily encouragement, moral support, and good cheer of my wife of nearly fifty years. This work is as much a testament to her personal fortitude, patience, and wisdom as it is to my good fortune. Being immeasurably grateful to her understates my everlasting thankfulness for her reassuring presence.

I have tried to exercise care and good judgment in presenting the evidence. Where I have failed, the blame rests solely on me.

Index